Living in France

ASSOCIATION OF AMERICAN WIVES OF EUROPEANS - B.P. 127 - 92154 SURESNES CEDEX - TÉL. : (1) 47.28.46.39

AAWE *Living in France*
Association of American Wives of Europeans
Paris, 1993

Publication Director: Carolyn White-Lesieur

Editor: Alexandra Boutin
Publication Assistants: Lynne Chaillat, 1990-1, Anne-Marie Leroy, 1991-2

JOB-HUNTING IN FRANCE: Pamela Perraud

DIVORCE IN FRANCE: Carla Potok

Contributions from Persis Gouirand, Ellen Grandsard, Judy Stewart-Vidal
Edited by Alexandra Boutin

RETIREMENT IN FRANCE Section One: Phyllis Michaux , Marilyn Gillet
Section Two: Benoit Besson

Edited by Daniel Beaudet, Lois Beaudet, Peter Kenton, Carolyn White-Lesieur

---

WILLS AND INHERITANCE: Persis Gouirand

Contributions from Sam Okoshken, Esq.

Technical assistance: Susan Besson, Alexandra Boutin, Susan Dalipagic,
Kathy Fabre, Persis Gouirand, Rae Leffman

Computer assistance was provided by :
  Microsoft
          Michel Lironcourt, MBL Consultants
              Barbara Sprzeuzkouski
                  Irene Checler
                  Lionel Roufosse

Proofreaders: Lois Beaudet, Lynn Beaudet, Phyllis Barbe, Alexandra Boutin,
Kathleen de Carbuccia, Persis Gouirand, Rhoda Seidler

Public Relations: Sally Lefèvre

AAWE cannot be held responsible for any information contained in or omitted from this book. The reader is advised to seek professional counsel for the elaboration or verification of any legal point treated herein. This book is intended for the general public and is not for professional use.

AAWE Living in France

Table of Contents

Foreword
Acknowledgements

FOREWORD

The Association of American Wives of Europeans is a non-profit organization that was founded in 1961 by Phyllis Michaux. Its members are, for the most part, permanent residents of France.

As a service to AAWE members and other residents of the English-speaking community in France, AAWE Living in France will attempt to explain some of the basic and some of the more complicated elements of the topics selected: job-hunting, divorce, retirement and inheritance in France.

Hopefully, once readers understand the major concepts, they will be in a better position to undertake further research. To familiarize readers with the language they will encounter in such research, we have used French terms with explanations in English throughout the texts. This guide is intended for the general public and not for professional use.

Carolyn White-Lesieur

Acknowledgements

The <u>AAWE Living in France</u> book has been over three years in the making. It came about in this way: AAWE had provided a service to the community with the <u>AAWE Guide to Education</u>. There are a lot of clever women in AAWE. Weren't there other topics of interest to permanent, English-speaking residents in France about which AAWE members could research and write? Their efforts would enable the association to render a service to the community, just the way it has done in the past, particularly on the subject of U.S. citizenship of bicultural children. We, as permanent residents of France, seemed capable of undertaking such a project.

Once we had picked the topics, **Lynne Chaillat** got the project off the ground. She found most of the authors and kept in touch with them to check on progress.

Phyllis Michaux and **Marilyn Gillet** finished their document on retirement in record time. In fact, Phyllis said she put it in a drawer and forgot about it!

We wanted some details on what one can do at age forty to prepare for retirement. A member's husband, **Benoit Besson** observed that he had the knowledge we were seeking on the French retirement system and investments. He believes, as we do, in altruism so he sat down and wrote and wrote and **Susan Besson**, his wife, typed and typed.

Persis Gouirand offered to do Wills and Retirement because of a personal interest in the subject. She was anxious to see the section in print so we made a special printing which sold out in fifteen minutes at Sam Okoshken's lecture last year.

Pam Perraud finished "Job-Hunting in Paris" which a few of us have already tested: her no frills, succinct document is 100% fact and 100% helpful.

Is it any surprise that the subject of divorce took the longest to complete? We had a few false starts. **Judy Stewart-Vidal** produced a fine article but admitted that she wasn't a lawyer and suggested a lawyer be consulted.

At the same time, **Anne-Marie Leroy** took over from **Lynne Chaillat.** We were fortunate to find an AAWE member, lawyer **Carla Potok,** who was willing to spend much time on the legal aspects. Doing this while having a full-time practice and family was no mean feat. **Ellen Grandsard** contributed valuable information on the helpful tool of Divorce Mediation and, once again, **Persis Gouirand** lent her skill at fact-finding and double-checking useful addresses and resources. I gathered the commentaries as I felt personal views of divorce by those who have experienced it might be eye-openers for those considering it. I'm grateful to those people who contributed a commentary. It's not always pleasant to reminisce about a conflictual period of one's life which one might prefer to forget.

Several people came forward to help with the typing: **Rae Leffman** typed half of the manuscript. **Kathy Fabre, Susan Besson, Sandy Boutin, Persis Gouirand** and myself typed the rest. **Lionel Roufosse** transformed a few diskettes for us saving someone (me!) from retyping a lot of pages.

Every single page was edited by **Sandy Boutin**. Nothing escaped her eye and way with words.

All of the authors helped proofread their own articles. Then **Sandy Boutin, Phyllis Barbe, Lois Beaudet, Rhoda Seidler** poured over the texts to find misspelled words and forgotten letters or words. **Kathleen de Carbuccia, Susan Besson, Daniel Beaudet, Lynn Beaudet** (a family affair!), **Peter Kenton** and **Carla Potok** also reviewed sections prior to publication.

Carol Maréchal and **Margee Dickason** helped **Anne-Marie Leroy** with obtaining printers' estimates, and **Barbara Brechet** handled advertising.

Microsoft gave us their support by offering a software program. Their instant reply was proof that this project was worth pursuing even if it did seem endless.

Michel Lironcourt and **MBL Consultants** showed their support by loaning a portable computer. They also imparted precious tips and computer help when necessary.

Irene Checler and **Barbara Sprzeuzkouski** gave time and expertise as generously as ever.

Although mentioned earlier for her editing skills, **Sandy Boutin** was always there at the other end of the phone for numerous consultations and requests for advice: she has been the rock of Gibraltar. Her efficiency, speed and wise advice made this a most enjoyable project to work on together.

I extend thanks to everyone for all their help, enthusiasm, and patience but especially to **Sandy Boutin, Lynne Chaillat, Phyllis Barbe, Persis Gouirand** and **Lois Beaudet (and family)** for believing in this project as much as I and never being too busy to lend a hand.

Carolyn White-Lesieur
March, 1993

AAWE members who contributed to AAWE Living in France:

Michael Adler	Ellen Grandsard
Phyllis Barbe	Peter Kenton
Roberta Beardsley	Rae Leffman
Lois Beaudet	Julie Lemoine
Susan Besson	Anita Mallick
Alexandra Boutin	Carol Maréchal
Barbara Brechet	Anne-Marie Leroy
Sandra Caillens Freland	Phyllis Michaux
Kathleen de Carbuccia	Pam Perraud
Lynne Chaillat	Carla Potok
Irene Checler	Marissa Roufosse
Susan Dalipagic	Rhoda Seidler
Margee Dickason	Barbara Sprzeuzkouski
Laura Dondey	Judy Stewart-Vidal
Kathy Fabre	Virginia Vittoz
Marilyn Gillet	Harriet Welty Rochefort
Persis Gouirand	Carolyn White-Lesieur

plus 9 people who contributed anonymous divorce commentaries

Non-AAWE members

Daniel Beaudet
Lynn Beaudet
Benoit Besson
Michel Lironcourt, MBL Consultants
Microsoft
Sam Okoshken
Lionel Roufosse

JOB - HUNTING IN PARIS

by

Pamela B. Perraud

ABOUT THE AUTHOR

PAMELA B. PERRAUD is a native of Minneapolis. A Connecticut College graduate, she holds two graduate degrees, including one in business. She has worked as a personnel consultant to an agency of the U.S. Embassy in Paris, as a recruiter for IBM Europe and as a professor at several business schools in Paris, including the American Business School, Institut Supérieur de Gestion and H.E.C. She has also run workshops in job-hunting techniques in Paris, London and the USA.

She became an AAWE member after her marriage to a Frenchman in 1975. In 1992, she became President of WICE.

JOB-HUNTING IN PARIS by Pamela B. Perraud
TABLE OF CONTENTS

I. INTRODUCTION

Looking for a job anywhere is always a difficult task. Job-hunting in a foreign city is even more daunting. Half the battle is knowing what to expect and where to begin.

The information given here is designed for the English-speaking person who is just starting his/her job hunt in Paris. I offer the following tips as a good starting point and hope you will find them useful.

Pamela B. Perraud, Paris 1993

➜   Note: New opportunities may soon be available in American Consulates and Embassies. As we go to press, the Department of State is drawing up guidelines to implement legislation sponsored by Senator Rockefeller and passed by Congress in 1991, which will provide for the local hiring of U.S. citizens.

It is to be hoped that under the guidelines, Americans will no longer be excluded from the many positions now filled by host country and third country nationals.

II. THE FRENCH JOB MARKET

A. REALITIES

* You should recognize that France, like most other industrialized countries, has a significant unemployment problem.

* The French are nationalistic and reason that a French person should be hired before a foreigner.

* You really must learn the language well if you hope to get a good job in France or if you hope to have a choice in the job you want. There are some exceptions to this rule, but they are few and far between.

* Unless you are totally bilingual, a French native will speak better French than you. Present other skills to a future employer in order to successfully compete against a local person.

* In your home territory, under the best of circumstances, any job search will take a great deal of time, effort, research and contacts. Assume that it will take twice the time, effort, research and contacts to land the job you want in Paris.

* Don't become discouraged. There are jobs available out there. If you are really having no luck after several months, you may have to re-evaluate your goals, your techniques and become more flexible in terms of the type of job you seek.

B. LEGALITIES OF WORKING IN FRANCE

In order to work in France you must have permission from the government. The French make a distinction between permission to reside in France and permission to work. All foreigners who are given permission to temporarily reside in France are not necessarily entitled to work in France.

The regulations regarding the right to work for foreigners are complex and ever-changing. At the present time the rules include the following:

IF YOU ARE MARRIED TO A FRENCH NATIONAL - You may apply for a 10-year *Carte de Résident* entitling you to work and reside in France. You may apply for this at your nearest *préfecture* (see list which follows). Note: a law requiring a one-year waiting period after the marriage for the right to work has been recently repealed.

IF YOU ARE AN EEC NATIONAL - No special permits are required.

IF YOU ARE MARRIED TO AN EEC NATIONAL - You are entitled to a 5-year *Carte de Séjour Salarié*. This will allow you to work anywhere in France. While your EEC spouse did not apply for any special permit, the non-EEC partner must apply at the nearest French consulate. Note: spouses of Spanish or Portuguese nationals will not be entitled to this privilege until Spain and Portugal are full members of the EEC.

MEMBER OF THE BRITISH COMMONWEALTH - Although British nationals need no special permits, citizens of Commonwealth nations (Australia, New Zealand, Canada, for example) must apply for working papers and a *Carte de Séjour,* as do other foreign nationals.

OTHER CASES - For people in other categories, the right to work is determined by other criteria, for example:

- why you came to France (to study, to visit, etc.)
- how long you plan to be in France (less than 3 months, more than 6 months, permanently)
- your financial resources as well as the salary level you are seeking
- whether you already have a specific job offer

Depending upon your own circumstances, you may or may not be entitled to a work permit. For full information about whether you qualify and the procedures to follow, contact *La Direction Départementale du Travail et de l'Emploi* at your nearest *préfecture.*

Paris (75) - Tel: 42.33.51.26.
Hauts-de-Seine (92) - Nanterre - Tel: 47.25.95.33.
Yvelines (78) - Préfecture Versailles - Tel: 39.51.99.33.
Val-de-Marne (94) - Créteil - Tel: 48.98.92.15.

FOR ADDITIONAL INFORMATION IN ENGLISH - Contact:

WICE - 20, boulevard Montparnasse, Paris 75015 Tel: 45.66.75.50.

Periodically WICE offers information sessions in English on everything you need to know about obtaining working papers. Lectures include how to apply for papers as well as recent changes in legislation.

IF YOU ARE NOT ELIGIBLE FOR A FRENCH WORK PERMIT:

If you cannot work legally in France, there are still other ways to utilize your time and talents. You might consider starting your own business if you plan to be here for a long time, or you might consider volunteering your time.

Volunteering is an excellent way to utilize your talents while you learn French, make contacts and get acclimated to France. See section on opportunities for volunteering in Paris.

III. SELF-ASSESSMENT AND MAKING AN ACTION PLAN

WHERE ARE YOU GOING?

Starting out on a job hunt without a clear idea of what you want is like starting on a trip without a road map or even a destination. If you do not have a road map as well as a destination clearly chosen, how will you ever know where you are going, or worse yet, how will you know when you have arrived?

A. SELF- ASSESSMENT: WHAT DO YOU HAVE TO OFFER?

1. General advice - Whether you are looking for a job in Paris, Tokyo or London, you must begin the job-hunting process by taking a good look at yourself. It is a pencil and paper task. You need to ask yourself some very pertinent questions.

2. Questions to ask:

* What specific skills and/or job experience do I have to offer?

* What are my strengths?

* What are my weaknesses?

* What types of job responsibilities am I able to handle?

* What is the level of real commitment I am willing to make to a future employer?

B. GOAL-SETTING: WHAT DO YOU WANT?

1. Once you have determined what you have to offer an employer, you then have to ask yourself what you want out of a job.

2. What would be your "ideal" or "dream" job in France? What is your ultimate goal?

3. Questions to answer:

* What types of working conditions are you looking for?

* Hours (full-time? part-time?)

* Location (commuting time?)

* Salary: base salary vs. take-home pay (*brut* vs. *net*), tax considerations?

* What are your long- and short-term employment goals?

* Are you looking for a "career" post or "just a job"?

* How "meaningful" does the job have to be?

* For what type of company and/or organization do you want to work?

4. Interviewing material - You are not ready to begin until you have answers to all these questions. These are exactly the same questions a prospective employer will ask on your first interview.

5. Focusing on what you want - You will not have any idea where to begin your job hunt without focusing specifically on your ultimate goal.

6. Flexibility - These job goals should not be written in stone. You can always make slight adjustments and modifications as the circumstances dictate. However, consider your self-assessment as the first step in a longer, more in-depth goal-setting process.

C. MAKING AN ACTION PLAN: <u>HOW ARE YOU GOING TO PROCEED?</u>

Once your goal - or destination - is set, you must make a plan on how to proceed. You need a road to get there. This plan will be your job hunt road map. You should set deadlines to complete each task. A complete "Employment Action Plan" should include:

* Preparing C.V. and cover letters
* Practicing interview questions
* Anticipating employment tests
* Contacting public and private sources of employment information
* Compiling lists of firms to contact
* Compiling lists of friends and associates to contact
* Networking possibilities in Paris
* Spending plenty of time preparing your "employment package".

The timetable should be reasonable:
* 1. You should be well-prepared before you make the first contact.
* 2. Do not try to plan too many interviews the same day. It is better to space the interviews with plenty of time to prepare and "recover".
* 3. Realize that a thorough job-hunt can take several months; rarely is your "destination" reached in a few weeks.

IV. PREPARING YOUR EMPLOYMENT PACKAGE

A. RESUMES/CURRICULA VITAE

The French C.V. follows the same basic principles as the American/British C.V. Its main purpose is to summarize what one has to offer an employer in terms of education, experience, and skills. A C.V. must be typed in correct French on high quality paper. Do not try to use a fancy format. In France, it is better to be conservative. If possible, have a native speaker review the French before you start to send the C.V. out to companies.

1. BASIC CONTENTS - The following items must be included in a C.V. in France.

NAME
ADDRESS
TELEPHONE
EDUCATION
WORK EXPERIENCE
PERSONAL INTERESTS
SKILLS (including LANGUAGES and COMPUTER SKILLS)
MARITAL STATUS
AGE
NATIONALITY
MILITARY SERVICE

EXPLANATION OF THE KEY ITEMS

TELEPHONE NUMBER - Most initial contacts are made by telephone. If you will not always be at home waiting by the telephone, leave the number of a friend or get an answering machine. Have a clear succinct message without background music. If you wish to be considered "professional", sound professional.

EDUCATIONAL BACKGROUND - You must realize that the French are preoccupied with credentials, so do not neglect this section. As a matter of fact, it should be listed prominently. List schools and/or training only after the secondary level. Do try to explain your diplomas in terms of French equivalents if you know them. Your future employers may ask you to produce copies of your diplomas, so have copies available but do not mail them.

Names and dates of schools and/or employment should appear in reverse chronological order in order to emphasize your most recent experience. Do list years and major field of studies, but do not list your courses. Don't list your grade-point average. List only major honors.

WORK EXPERIENCE - Be sure to list the following: job title, company name, city (the actual street address is not necessary; save this information for your list of references), employment dates (months and years), as well as a quick summary of duties. Do not list on the C.V. why you left, your previous salary or any of your references.

Cite whenever possible your specific accomplishments in your previous positions. You may list part-time and volunteer work, as well. Relevant experience is what counts more than whether you were paid for it. Ordinarily jobs are listed in reverse chronological order (most recent first); however, you may use different types of formats (See sample C.V. after this section).

SKILLS - List your language skills, beginning with French. Be honest about your level. Your weaknesses will become apparent immediately. Also, be sure to list any computer skills. Skip your typing skills if you do not want a job where you are required to type.

PERSONAL INTERESTS - This is often included in French C.V.'s Only list serious hobbies. Avoid listing frivolous items such as baton-twirling, etc.

MARITAL STATUS - This is a tricky issue with many employers, since the categories - "married, single, divorced or widowed" - evoke different reactions in different types of people and for different types of jobs. It is best to skip this item completely. Never list children or their ages on a C.V.

PHOTOS - Pictures are often requested. You do not have to send a photo. Advice:- do not send one unless it is absolutely required for a job such as modeling or an acting position where your physical appearance is very important.

REFERENCES - You should not list references on the actual C.V. You may need a list of them to refer to in order to complete an application form, so have one handy. Try to give as references people who have worked with you or know your professional skills.

SPECIAL ITEMS - There are several items which must be included in a French C.V. which normally are not included in C.V. in other countries:

    * AGE - In the U.S., for example, it is suggested that one avoid stating one's age. In France, it is a necessity. Your C.V. will be regarded with suspicion if you do not include it. Omission only leads to problems.

    * NATIONALITY - This should be clearly stated on your C.V. Always mention that you have working papers, otherwise you may be rejected on this basis alone. If you have French dual nationality, state it. It can help.

2. FORMATS

There are three basic types of formats for C.V.:

Chronological,
Functional and
Mixed (examples are shown in the appendix)

a. CHRONOLOGICAL

This format is the most classical and probably the most acceptable for the French market. Luckily, it is also the easiest to prepare.

You list your employment and/or experiences in chronological order. List your most recent job first. The major disadvantage of this format is the fact that you risk highlighting your most recent job experience which may or may not be what you want to emphasize.

For example, while your real interest is marketing, your most recent job was as a sales clerk. Unfortunately that was the only job you could find at the time. That sales job will stick out prominently on your C.V. and you will have to do a lot of explaining to a prospective employer if you wish to go into a responsible position in the marketing field.

b. FUNCTIONAL

This is a way of organizing the C.V. to emphasize your qualifications or special interests without necessarily explaining when these skills were acquired.

In other words, you highlight everything you want and leave out items that may not "fit" into the job or career you envisage. Hence, if you have any "gaps" they will not be as apparent as in the chronological C.V.

The disadvantage of this type of format is that often the employers are uncomfortable with it and assume the candidate is hiding something by not placing job experience in chronological order.

c. MIXED

This is a combination of the chronological and functional formats. You highlight areas of expertise that you want the employer to see and at the same time, include names, dates and places of employment in chronological order. You do this in a way to accentuate your best qualities for the specific job in question. This provides more flexibility in presentation.

B. COVER LETTERS: BASICS

1. Purpose - The purpose of the cover letter is to introduce yourself to the prospective employer, to state why you are interested in the particular job/company, and to create enough interest in you on the part of the employer so that you are invited for an interview.

2. Writing - Traditionally in France, a cover letter (*lettre de candidature*) is handwritten, rather than typewritten. Since over 80% of national companies recently surveyed in France said they use graphology (handwriting analysis) as part of the recruitment process, it is extremely important how you write and prepare your letter. You will be judged on both the content and the appearance.

3. Appearance

    a. Use only top quality 80 gram, unlined white paper.

    b. Use a fountain pen. Many French companies do not consider a ballpoint pen"proper" for a formal letter.

    c. Be sure to write a draft first so that the text is well-centered on the page.

    d. Try to write at your natural speed.

    e. Have a native speaker check and proofread the French text.

    f. Remember that graphologists will check the envelope so copy the address carefully. Have it neatly written on the envelope.

4. Addressing your Letter

    a. Be sure to send the letter to the proper person. If you are applying in response to an advertisement, send your letter to the person listed in the advertisement. Otherwise, try to find the name of the person who is in charge of the specific department for which you wish to work.

    b. You can usually obtain the name by calling the main switchboard of the company and asking for the department director's name. This quick phone call will save you a great deal of time because your C.V. will land on the right desk.

    c. Do not necessarily assume you should send your letter to the personnel office. Most personnel offices are notorious in not sending along interesting C.V.'s to other departments seeking new staff members.

5. Content

    a. Try to begin by stating why you are writing to this particular company or organization. For example, note whether you were referred by someone or saw an advertisement. If referring to an advertisement, be sure to note the reference number because many large companies run several different types of ads the same day.

"Votre offre d'emploi dans le Figaro le 4 juin a retenu toute mon attention. Cela correspond à ce que je cherche actuellement...."

"Mme Sophie Dupont, qui travaille pour votre compagnie à New York, m'a conseillé de vous contacter....."

    b. State what you feel you have to offer the company in one or two sentences. Do not re-state everything that you put on the C.V. This is your chance to make a specific pitch for a particular type of job. This is perhaps the most important sentence of the whole letter.

Examples:

"Je possède quatre ans d'experience dans ......"
"Pour ma part, j'ai eu la responsabilité de ...."

6. Conclusion/Opening for interview

a. Your last paragraph should state when you would be available for
   interviews.

b. Don't be either too timid or too aggressive in your tone and make sure it
   includes a proper French closing.

Examples:

*"Je me tiens à votre disposition pour un entretien et vous prie d'agréer, Monsieur,
l'assurance de mes sentiments devoués."*

*"Dans l'attente de vous rencontrer, je vous prie d'agréer, Monsieur le chef du
personnel, l'assurance de mes sentiments distingués."*

7. Length

Keep it short. Maximum 4 or 5 paragraphs. See sample letters in the
Appendix.

C. PREPARING THE INTERVIEW

The interview is the "acid" test as to whether or not you get the job. The interviewer
wants to see what you really have to offer and how well you present yourself. For the
foreigner, this will be the real test of how well one speaks French. As in any other interview
situation, practicing and anticipating the questions is the best way to prepare for the interview.

Remember the interview starts at the door. The secretary may watch you while you are
in the waiting room. So, act poised and confident.

1. BASICS- A couple of other hints:

APPEARANCE- The importance of your appearance can not be
stressed enough. You must look clean and polished from head to toe. In France, it is best to
risk being considered too dressy than too casual.

Women should wear something simple - a suit or plain dress. Nothing
fussy, clinging, low-cut or trendy.
Avoid clanking jewelry, big hats, wild stockings, strong perfume, etc.
Moderation is the "watch" word.
Men - simple suit and tie. A tie is a must.

PROMPTNESS - You should arrive at least 10-15 minutes early. This gives you plenty of time to calm down, collect your thoughts and survey the office.
Expect to wait. Remember that they assume their time is more valuable than yours.

PREPARATION -
* Do research on the company and/or organization - find out as much as you can about their product/service etc.

* Try to anticipate the questions you will be asked. Practice with a native speaker.

* Plan to ask some questions of your own about the company, the hours, the working conditions, etc.
* Bring along another copy of your C.V., photocopies of your diplomas (often requested in France), a list of former job references (names), samples of your work if you are an artist, photographer or designer.

BODY LANGUAGE - Remember that body gestures give clues about your character and/or your attitude.

* Try to appear relaxed (even though you are not).

* Do not slouch or fidget in your chair. If you do not know what to do with your hands, fold them in your lap or keep them next to you.

* Do not bring pencils, cigarettes or other objects to the interview.

* Appear interested and alert. Pay attention to the questions.

* Look the person in the eye.

* Give the interviewer a firm handshake.

ANSWERING QUESTIONS - Be careful of how you answer and what you say. Make sure your answers are clear and distinct. Avoid answering just "yes" or "no". Also avoid long-winded answers that put the interviewer to sleep.

* Never lie. Any falsehood will come back to haunt you. Better to avoid a subject than to lie about it.

* Never say anything bad about a former employer. Assume your references will be checked.

* Never lose your temper. Some employers try to use "pressure" interviews to see how you will react. Don't fall for this ploy. Keep your cool no matter what is said.
* Remain positive.

THINGS TO AVOID

* Do not oversell yourself. Some people do not know when to quit. You are expected to discuss your accomplishments; however, try to stop short of being considered a braggart or an egotist.

* Do not dwell on salary/benefits. Of course, salary and benefits are very important considerations for any job; however, try not to overdo, particularly in the first interview or the interviewer will assume that is all you are interested in.

Let the interviewer bring up the subject of salary first. If you are interested in a specific benefit package, ask the secretary in the personnel office for a brochure before you leave rather than taking up the time of your interviewer to discuss the pension plan.

BEST TIPS: **Always remain friendly yet businesslike.
\qquad\qquad **Stay alert and never let down your guard.
\qquad\qquad **Ask pertinent questions which show you are interested.

2. COMMON TYPES OF INTERVIEWS IN FRANCE

a. Simple Individual - The most common type is a one-on-one situation with a single interviewer asking all of the questions.

b. Interview by Jury - The individual is asked questions by a panel of people.

c. Successive - The person is individually interviewed by a series of people in the company.

d. Group Interview - Several candidates for one position are all interviewed at the same time, often around a small table, to see how they compare with one another.

3. TYPICAL INTERVIEW QUESTIONS ASKED

Pourquoi posez-vous votre candidature à ce poste?
(Why are you applying for this job?)

Quelle est votre formation?
(What is your education/training?)

Quelle est votre expérience?
(What is your experience in the field?)

Pour quelle raison avez-vous quitté votre employeur?
(Why did you leave your last job?)

Où avez-vous le mieux réussi? Pourquoi?
(Where were your greatest successes? Why?)

Quels sont vos objectifs professionels?
(What are your professional objectives?)

Connaissez-vous notre entreprise?
(Do you know our company?)

Pourquoi voulez-vous changer de métier?
(Why do you want to change your career?)

Savez-vous travailler en équipe?
(Do you know how to work on a team?)

Savez-vous prendre des initiatives?
(Do you know how to take the initiative?)

Etes-vous mariée? Avez-vous des enfants?
(Are you married? Do you have children?)

Comment pensez-vous concilier vie familiale et vie professionelle?
(How do you think you can reconcile family and professional life?)

Quelles sont vos prétentions?
(What kind of salary are you looking for?)

Quelles sont vos points faibles?
(What are your weak points?)

Quelles sont vos points forts?
(What are your strong points?)

Don't be surprised if you are asked highly personal questions that are legal for personnel people to ask in France, illegal in some other countries. For example:

Etes-vous enceinte?
(Are you pregnant?)

Etes-vous syndiquée?
(Are you a union member?)

The question you want to hear is *"A partir de quand seriez-vous disponible?"* ("When are you available to start work?")

D. EMPLOYMENT TESTS

In most large French corporations and many smaller companies, pre-employment tests are very common. There are basically three types:

1. Aptitude Tests - These are basically designed to test your logic, speed and intelligence. They usually consist of number sequences, dominos, designs or "complete the phrase" - type tests. Obviously, the foreigner is at a severe disadvantage in the literary/language tests. Do not forget to point this out to the person testing you. Ask questions if you do not understand what is being asked.

2. Personality Tests - These are supposed to discover your true personality traits and can run the gamut from the ridiculous to the sublime. They might include personality inventories, situational choices, Rorschach ink blots, tree-designing, playing with blocks, and creating dialogues between characters in a situation.

3. Language Tests - If you are a foreigner applying for a job in a multi-national corporation or international agency, you might be required to take a language test to prove your language skills. So, be prepared.

Several good books can be found on the market to prepare for these tests, including:

*_Reussir les Tests d'Entreprise_ by Gilles Azzopardi, Marabout, ed. 1983 and
*_Pour Maîtriser les Tests de Recrutement_ by Anne Bacus, Marabout, ed. 1990.

GENERAL TIPS FOR TESTING

* As in all testing, try to remain calm.

* For the personality tests: always go for the "golden mean."

* Never choose the extremes in any situation and remember: you love your mother, but not too much; you love your father, but not too much. These tests look for aberrations, not the commonplace. Do not try to guess what they are trying to find out. You may be wrong.

V. TAPPING RESOURCES IN PARIS

A. PUBLIC AGENCIES

France has created many specialized agencies to assist job hunters. When you need advice choose the one that best suits your own situation.

1. ANPE (*Agence Nationale pour l'Emploi*) under the Ministry of Social Affairs and Employment

The services of this agency are open to all people eligible to work in France. You can register for assistance if you are unemployed or if you wish to change jobs. The services the ANPE offers include giving information on job openings, as well as information on training or traineeship opportunities. You can also use its extensive information services and counseling services.

The ANPE also offers:

S.O.A. (*Session d'Orientation Approfondie*) - a fifty-hour course on job orientation and job hunting techniques.

T.R.E. (*Techniques de Recherche d'Emploi*) - a short two-day course on job hunting hints.

E.N.C.P. (*Evaluation du Niveau de Compétences Professionnelles*) - This is a special type of test to evaluate skills and experience, designed for people who have either been out of the job market for some time or whose diplomas are not necessarily adequate for jobs sought. This test gives a nationally recognized certificate of educational equivalency.

LOCATIONS: There are ANPE's located in all major cities in France and throughout the Paris region. You may find your local ANPE by contacting the "*Mairie*" or by looking in the Yellow Pages of the telephone directory under "*Administrations du Travail et de l'Emploi.*"

Centers for *cadres* only:

The ANPE has special centers in Paris that handle only the "*cadre*" or "white collar/manager" level jobs, specifically for those who have a university diploma. Those centers handle people based upon where they live in Paris. They include:

ANPE - 1*, 2*, 3*, 4*, 5*, 12*, 13*, 14*
12, rue Moulin des Prés
75013 Paris
Tel: 45.80.41.21.

ANPE - 6*, 7*, 8*, 15*
43, rue de Javel
75015 Paris
Tel: 45.77.59.56.

ANPE - 9*, 16*, 17*
12, rue Blanche
75009 Paris
Tel: 42.85.44.40.

ANPE - 10*, 11*, 18*, 19*, 20*
70, rue Crimée
75019 Paris
Tel: 42.01.42.00.

(* = *arrondissement*)

2. *AFPA* (*Cercle de Recherche Actif*): 94, rue Jean-Pierre Timbaud, 75011 Paris; Tel: 43.55.53.75. and another at 51, rue de la Glaciere, 75013 Paris; Tel: 43.41.28.18.

This organization, part of the ANPE, gives a special three-week training program, free of charge, covering job-hunting techniques. It acts as a job club helping job seekers.

3. *C.I.O.* (*Centre d'information et d'orientation*)

The C.I.O. is part of the Ministry of National Education and provides information on schools, professions and national tests. This is a good place to inquire about specific educational requirements for professions and where specialized training is offered.

LOCATIONS: Inquire at the local *Mairie* for addresses of local CIO's. Each school district has one, as do many universities.

4. *C.N.I.D.F.F.* (*Centre National d'Information et de Documentation des Femmes et des Familles*)

These are centers designed to give women information about training and local job opportunities as well as information on many other topics including the rights of women in France with regards to marriage, divorce and taxes. For job-hunting purposes, they give information for women returning to the world of work and some assistance in job referrals. They publish several useful books related to job-hunting:

"*La Recherche d'Emploi*", "*Droits du Travail - Les Femmes Salariées*" and "*Passeport pour la Formation Professionnelle*"

LOCATIONS: Contact CNIDFF: 7 rue de Jura, 75013 Paris; Tel: 43.31.12.34. for the location of the nearest CNIDFF. There are about 200 centers in France.

B. PRIVATE ORGANIZATIONS

1. *A.P.E.C.* (*Association Pour l'Emploi des Cadres*)
51, blvd Brune, 75014 Paris; Tel: 40.52.20.00.

This is an organization formed by national employers and unions to work in conjunction with the ANPE to find jobs for "*cadre*-level" people. The services are free and open to employed or unemployed managers. There is a very good "*salle d'auto-documentation*" (reading room with plenty of information, newspapers, a bulletin board with job offers, etc.) If you register with the A.P.E.C., you receive a weekly magazine called "*Courrier Cadre*" which gives job listings and information on the job market. Job counselors are seen by appointment only.

2. MIRP 5, rue Roquépine, 75008 Paris; Tel: 42.66.09.83.

This non-profit organization helps people to find employment.on an individual basis It is geared only to those who have been unemployed for over six months. The service is free. Clients must call for an individual interview.

3. *Retravailler* - 34, rue Balard, 75015 Paris; Tel: 45.58.23.09.

This non-profit organization is designed to help women between the ages of 25-55 who have been out of the job market for some time. It organizes a special training course which lasts five weeks and is offered about five times a year in Paris. The course covers an evaluation of current skills, possible careers, orientation to the local job market and job-hunting techniques. Like the ANPE, they also offer S.O.A.'s for seven days in groups of about ten people. The costs vary according to the client's circumstances.

4. *Centre Varenne* - 18, rue de Varenne, 75007 Paris; Tel: 42.22.18.56.

This is a private organization that offers job-hunting help and seminars twice a week from 9a.m. - noon. There are usually about ten to twelve people in the group, and the price is about 200FF.

5. *AVARAP* - 9, rue Emile Duclaux, 75015 Paris; Tel: 45.60.03.33.

This private, non-profit organization helps professional level people (*cadres*) "re-orient" themselves and encourages them to look for jobs. It works with the ANPE as well as with individuals. The basic cost is about 400 FF per year.

6. *La Pêche des Chomeurs* - 123, rue Jacques Coeur, 75004 Paris;
Tel: 48.04.06.44.

This is a very unique 10-day free program which tries to encourage job hunters by rebuilding their confidence using acting methods. The program is given about six times a year in Paris as well as in other locations all over France. About forty-sixty people attend each class.

C. NEWSPAPERS

You should realize that 80% or more of the jobs available are never advertised in any newspaper; they are filled by word-of-mouth. However, newspapers are a great source of information about who is hiring, salary rates, and names of contacts. Obviously, it is a good place to run advertisements for yourself. Occasionally you can even find jobs through newspapers, so don't overlook them, particularly the specialized newspapers, if you have a specialized skill.

English Language Newspapers:

The Herald Tribune: Tel: 46.37.93.00. - Check for daily ads. Numerous teaching jobs are advertised. It is also a great place to run your own advertisement.
France-USA Contacts (FUSAC): Tel: 43.26.87.83. Another good place to run your own advertisement. This magazine appears in the U.S. as well as in France. A copy can be found in most American organizations in Paris such as churches, restaurants, library, etc.

French Language Newspapers

Regular mass media

	Best day to look at job section
France-Soir	Monday
Le Figaro	Monday
Le Monde	Monday/Wednesday for engineers, managers; Wednesday for computer people
Les Echos	Monday
Liaisons Sociales (for social science and personnel jobs)	

Weekly magazines

Le Point	Mondays
L'Express	Fridays
L'Expansion	Fridays

Specialized newspapers/magazines

Les Annonces	Mondays
Le Marché du Travail	Mondays
Stratégies	(for media and advertising)
Zéro 1	(for computer technicians)
Courrier Cadre	available from APEC
Le JOB	available from APEC
Le Journal du Sefrane	(for jobs abroad)

D. MINITEL REFERENCES

Minitel, the French computer terminal network sponsored by France Telecom, is an easy way to obtain up-to-date information from your own home on job openings, salaries and all sorts of other references which could be useful in your job hunt. Some of the employment-related sources are:

3615 AC	*Action Emploi* - You may write your C.V. Put it on file for 15 days and it will be proposed to various organizations looking for employees with your qualifications. You can re-new after every 15 days.
3615 APEC	Listings of manager-level positions (*cadres*), updated daily.
3615 ARTG	Job listing service for professionals in graphic arts, advertising and communication.
3615 CRAC 3	Job listing service by regions in France as well as internationally.
3614 ECCO	Listing of the 400+ agencies who hire on a temporary basis.
3615 ICA	A bilingual listing of managerial-level jobs in France through a private headhunting agency.
3615 INDEP	Job listings in conjunction with the ANPE.
3616 INTERJOB	Job listings for temporary work all over France.
3615 LMI	Job ads from *Le Monde Informatique*.
3616 MANAGING	Job offers from a human resources firm.
3615 PSYCHOTEL	Ads for jobs for psychologists in France.
3615 SAGA	This service can give you an idea of the type of salary you can expect - factors include age, training, education and experience.
3616 SNCH	This service lists job announcements in the medical field.
3615 ULYSSE	THE master listing for *cadres* (managerial level jobs) in Paris. You will find everything here.

E. BULLETIN BOARDS

There are certain places in Paris where jobs for English-speaking people are posted other than in official French government agencies. Just a few of the most commonly used ones are listed below.

1. WICE - 20, bd. de Montparnasse, 75015 Paris; Tel: 45.66.75.50.
Jobs teaching English as well as some professional jobs are posted. There is also a professional bulletin board where business people may leave cards.

2. American Church- 65, quai d'Orsay, 75007 Paris; Tel: 47.05.07.99.
There is an official bulletin board for jobs on the ground floor; most of the jobs are for household help, au pair, etc. Occasionally, there are other, higher-level jobs posted. There are often notices in the basement for all sorts of odd jobs.

3. The British Institute - 11, rue de Constantine, 75007 Paris; Tel: 45.55.71.99.
There is a bulletin board listing some job openings for English-speaking people in Paris.

4. The American Library - 10, rue Général Camou, 75007 Paris;
          Tel: 45.55.91.73
There is a small bulletin board for job openings however, most are low-level odd jobs.

5. Business Schools - If you are interested in a traineeship, you should visit some of the business schools in Paris. Often employers contact the schools and request that traineeship offers be posted on their bulletin boards. The best school for top traineeship offers is HEC in Jouy-en Josas, Tel: 39.67.70.00.

F. TEMPORARY AGENCIES

A very good way for people to break into the French job market and/or for people returning to the job market after several years of absence is to try to get a job with a temporary agency, Such work is called "l'intérim".

Some of the other advantages of temporary work:
- It is a great way to get inside an organization to see if you really want to work there.
- You can get a variety of jobs in various offices and/or companies.
- You can refuse a job or stop temporarily, if you wish.
- Most of the better-known agencies such as Manpower and ECCO offer on-the-job training in computers, word processors, bookkeeping, etc.
- You get higher pay than for regular work in the same field because you receive a premium for taking short-term work.

The major disadvantages are:
- It is difficult to count on regular work.
- You start over every time you accept a new assignment.

G. HEADHUNTERS

Headhunters (*chasseurs de têtes*) are recruiting agents for companies. Usually, they are retained by major companies to recruit managers. They deal with all types of positions, but <u>not</u> at all levels.

Headhunters are highly selective. They are searching for candidates to fill <u>specific</u> vacancies. Your qualifications may or may not be what they are looking for at the moment. Normally, they like to do the asking so do not be surprised if you do not get any reply. However, most keep banks of resumes on file so you can always give them a try.

Listed below are some of the largest and best-known headhunters in Paris:

Heidrick and Struggles	6, Rond Point des Champs-Elysées, 75008 Paris Tel: 44.21.11.11.
Egon Zehnder	12, avenue Georges V, 75008 Paris, Tel: 44.31.81.00.
H. Neumann	120, avenue des Champs-Elysées, 75008 Paris Tel: 44.20.54.00.
R. Reynolds	7, place Vendôme, 75001 Paris Tel: 49.26.13.00.
Progress	57, avenue Franklin Roosevelt 75008 Paris Tel: 42.89.12.01.
Spencer Stuart	39, ave. Franklin Roosevelt 75008 Paris Tel: 45.62.62.20.
Leaders Trust Intl.	32, avenue Kléber 75116 Paris Tel: 45.02.17.00.
Korn Ferry	30, avenue Georges V, 75008 Paris Tel: 47.20.35.00.
Jouve & Assoc.	19, avenue Georges V, 75008 Paris Tel: 40.70.90.00.
Carre, Orban & Partners	166, rue du faubourg St. Honoré, 75008 Paris Tel: 42.25.87.23.

Note: For a complete listing of Paris headhunters with background information on the individual consultants, check the <u>1991 Consultex Guide to Choosing and Using a Headhunter in Europe, Vol. 1 - France.</u>

H. NETWORKING

"Networking" is the technique of making yourself known in the community. It is a way of marketing yourself and/or your skills. By networking, one attempts to meet a wider circle of professional acquaintances who will ,in turn, introduce you to other people. While networking has been around for years in the U.S., it is a relatively new phenomenon in Europe.

You can network by:
- Joining many of the clubs and organizations around Paris. (See "Volunteering Your Time".)
- Checking with the American Chamber of Commerce to see if your university has an alumni group in Paris.
- Joining one of the professional business groups in town.

In Paris, some of the best opportunities for business networking in English can be found through the following organizations:

- The American Club of Paris, 34, avenue de New York, 75016 Paris;
  Tel:47.23.64.36.

- Business Development Network International,
  c/o Elizabeth de Vulpillières,
  Parc Croix Marie, 4, avenue des Jonchères, 78121 Crespières,
  Tel: 30.54.94.66.

- American Chamber of Commerce, 21, ave. George V, 75008 Paris
  Tel: 47.23.70.28.

VI. TIPS FOR WOMEN RE-ENTERING THE WORK FORCE

1. Do not assume that your education and experience are worthless. Do try to attend a workshop on assessing your skills, interests and knowledge.

2. Do find out what skills are required in your field of interest and find out if you can get some re-training in your chosen field in France.

3. If you are not familiar with word-processing and general computer skills, take a basic course (see "Continuing Education").

4. Make sure you are really ready to go back to work. Can you answer the following questions?

> - Do you have back-up child care if the children get sick?
> - What about when the back-up person gets sick?
> - What about school vacations?
> - What about helping with homework?
>
> - Do you have other household help to take care of home duties?
>
> - Will you be able to work after hours if needed on a project at the office?
>
> - Can your husband, children, dog, cat, etc., really survive long hours without you?
>
> - If your husband is also working, have you calculated the actual cost/benefit of working? Have you considered the double social security charges and higher taxes?

5. In an interview situation, remember:

> - Do not stress your age; emphasize your maturity and experience.
>
> - Describe your time at home as a period durinig which you learned how to:
>> - manage your time as well as that of your husband and children
>> - organize a household
>> - juggle conflicting commitments
>> - handle crises
>> - manage a household budget

6. Consider using a "mixed" format for your C.V. rather than the "chronological" format which emphasizes employment "gaps".

VII. VOLUNTEERING YOUR TIME

For many people, volunteering is as useful a vocation as a paid job. Still others combine paid work with volunteer work. Luckily, there are many outlets for volunteering in Paris. It is an excellent way to pick up new job skills, learn the language better, and make good friends. Some great places to volunteer:

AAWE   Association of American Wives of Europeans
B.P. 127 , 92154 Suresnes Cedex, Tel. 47.28.46.39.

WICE   20, bd. du Montparnasse, 75015 Paris; Tel: 45.66.75.50.

American Aid Society- 2, ave. Gabriel, 75008 Paris; Tel: ~~42.96.12.02.~~ ~~ext. 2717~~

Adèle Annis 43.12.48.07

AARO   Association of Americans Resident Overseas
B.P. 127, 92154 Suresnes Cedex, Tel. 42.04.09.38.

AWG   American Women's Group
22bis, rue Pétrarque 75116 Paris; Tel: 47.55.87.50.

American Hospital   63, bd. Victor Hugo, 92200 Neuilly, Tel: 46.41.25.25.

Chébert 45.34.26.00

American Library   20, rue du Général Camou, 75007 Paris; Tel: 45.51.46.82.

American Church   65, quai d'Orsay, 75007 Paris; Tel: 47.05.07.99.

American Cathedral   23, ave. Georges V, 75008 Paris; Tel: 42.76.14.89.

BCWO   British Commonwealth Women's Organization
7, rue Auguste Vacquerie, 75016 Paris; Tel: 47.20.10.36.

Assoc. of Canadian   Canadian Cultural Center
Women   5, rue de Constantine, 75007 Paris

WFAA   World Federation of Americans Abroad *Umbrella Org.*
B.P. 127, 92154 Suresnes Cedex; Tel: 42.04.05.24.

Chairman of Directors ← Gregory Good   Helen Tagy
↳44.21.82.80
American Aid Society   Corporate Printing Co.
General   43.12.47.90

w/ AWE   Moira Clark 34.80.05.88
Andrew + Peggy Plessis 47.41.87.46

Sara Houiller # 39.12.09.80
Andrea Skudlark 39.73.10.76

VIII. CONTINUING EDUCATION

Another way to polish your skills before you go back to work or to keep yourself up-to-date is to take continuing education classes. Many opportunities exist to take classes in English as well as in French. In France, all employers must devote a certain percentage of their budget for "continuing education" (*la Formation Continue)*, so opportunities in French are plentiful. Check with your local *mairie* as well for continuing education classes.

For Classes in English, try:

WICE	20, bd. du Montparnasse, 75015 Paris; Tel: 45.66.75.50.
American University of Paris	31, ave. Bosquet, 75007 Paris; Tel: 45.55.91.73.
American Business School	15, ave. de la Grande Armée, 75116 Paris; Tel: 45.01.96.01
Hartford Business School	8, terrasse Bellini, La Défense, 92807 Puteaux, Tel: 49.00.19.61.
Boston University	Tour CIT, 3, rue de l'Arrivée, 75749 Paris Cedex 15, Tel: 43.35.00.60.
IEMI, St. Xavier	20, rue de St. Petersbourg, 75008 Paris; Tel: 42.93.13.87. ("rue de Leningrad" on old maps of Paris)

Other Institutions with Classes in English:

The Open University	28, rue du Four, 75006 Paris; Tel: 45.44.77.03.
European University	137, avenue Jean-Jaurès, 92140 Clamart; Tel: 46.44.39.39.
INSEAD	bd. de Constance, 77305 Fontainebleau; Tel: 60.72.40.00.
HEC/ISA	78350 Jouy-en-Josas, Tel: 39.56.73.56.

IX. GLOSSARY OF EMPLOYMENT TERMS

A
allocations de chômage:	unemployment payments
ancienneté:	seniority
annonces:	advertisements
apprentissage:	apprenticeship
avantages sociaux:	employee benefits

B
bénévole:	volunteer
bilan personnel:	personal inventory of skills
bulletin de paie:	official pay slip

C
cadre:	middle manager, white collar worker
candidature spontanée:	unsolicited application for a job
charges sociales:	social charges (government deductions on pay slip)
chasseur de têtes:	headhunter
chômage:	unemployment
compétence:	skill
concours:	competitive test or exam (usually refers to civil service)
congés:	paid leave time
congé de maternité:	maternity leave
contrat du durée déterminée:	fixed-term contracct (temporary)
contrat du durée indéterminée:	permanent contract
cotisations:	deductions - payments for social security and other funds

D
dactylographie:	typing
diplôme:	diploma or certificate
disponibilité:	availability for work
durée du travail:	working hours

E
embaucher:	to hire
entretien:	interview
équipe:	team (teamwork)
expérience professionnelle:	professional experience
expérience extra-professionnelle:	outside activities

F
formation:	education/training
formation continue:	continuing education

G
gestion:	management
graphologie:	handwriting analysis

H
horaires:	hours worked

I
informatique:	computer work
intérim:	temporary work

L

lettre de candidature:	cover letter
licencier:	to fire, dismiss
loisirs:	leisure-time activities (as a part of CV)

M

métier:	profession, line of work
mutation:	change of job or location

O

objectif professionnel:	professional objective (part of a CV)
objectif:	goal, objective
offre d'emploi:	job offer
organisation à but non-lucratif	non-profit organization

P

parrainage:	mentor, sponsorship
prétentions:	desired salary
primes:	special payments given for transportation, "13th month of salary"

R

recherche d'emploi:	job hunt
rémuneration:	payment received for work given

S

salaire de base:	base salary on which social charges are calculated
situation familiale:	marital status, children
SMIC:	minimum wage
stage:	traineeship
syndicat:	union

T

taches:	tasks, jobs
traitement de texte:	word processing
travail intermittent:	occasional work
travail partiel:	part-time work
travail plein temps:	full-time work
travailleur temporaire:	temporary worker

U

URSAAF:	agency where deducations for social security are sent for employees

V

violon d'Ingres:	one's hobby

X. BIBLIOGRAPHY

BOOKS ON JOB HUNTING TECHNIQUES IN FRANCE:

ADTS. *Comment Trouver un Emploi.* Paris: Editions ADTS, 1982

ANPE. *Guide de la Recherche d'Emploi.* Paris: ANPE, 1988

Bolles, Richard. *Chercheurs d'Emploi, N'Oubliez Pas Votre Parachute.* Paris: Sylvie Messinger, 1982 (Note: This is the French edition of the well-known book in U.S. with employment references for France)

Boutet, Jean-Patrick. *Chasseur d'Emploi.* Paris: First, Inc. Les Business Guides, 1988

Cadart, Nathalie. *Un Job sur Mesure.* Belgique: Marabout, 1988

CNIDFF. *La Recherche d'Emploi.* Paris: CNIDFF, 1986

STAFF. *Recruting Efficace.*: STAFF, Carnets de Recrutement, Nov. 1990

BOOKS ON WRITING A CURRICULUM VITAE:

Baden, Alain. *Le Guide Nouveau Curriculum Vitae.* Paris: Editions Fleurus, 1981

Huguet, Catherine. *Les Règles d'Or du Curriculum Vitae.* Alleur, Belgique: Marabout, 1985

Roudaut, Gérard. *Le Guide du C.V. Spécial Débutants.* Paris: Collections l'Etudiant Pratique, 1986

GUIDES FOR RESEARCHING JOBS AND/OR COMPANIES

American Chamber of Commerce. Guide to Members in France, published yearly. They also have listings of American firms in France and French firms in the U.S. Check with the Chamber for availability. Address: 21, avenue Georges V, 75008 Paris; Tel: 47.23.80.26.

Cadart, Nathalie. *Comment Devenir Fonctionnaire? Quel Employeur Choisir?* Paris: Marabout, 1986

Consultex: Choosing and Using a Headhunter in France by Nancy Garrison Jenn. Consultex, 1992

Didot Bottin. *Le Bottin Administratif Décentralisé*. This enormous directory of over 1400 pages has everything you want to know about all of the public services in France.

Didot Bottin. *Le Bottin Entreprises.* This has a listing of over 250,000 companies. This is about as complete a listing of companies in France as you will find anywhere including names of directors.
Both of the above Bottin directories should be consulted at an ANPE office or at Didot Bottin, 28, rue du Docteur Finlay, 75015 Paris; Tel:45.78.61.66.

Editions L'Etudiant. *Le Guide des Entreprises qui Recrutent.* Paris: 1988

Editions Formation - Carrières. *Le GO (Le Guide des Opportunités de Carrière)*. Paris, published annually

Fames International. *L'Annuaire au Feminin*. Puteaux: published annually

Loufrani, Jacky. *Manuel Méthodique pour une Préparation des Concours Administratifs*. **Paris: 1987**

Ministère des Affaires Etrangères. *Missions Diplomatiques en France*. **Paris: 1987**

Nouvel Economiste. *Le Carnet d'Adresses du Nouvel Economiste*. **Paris: 15, rue d'Uzes, 75063 Paris Cedex; Tel: 42.33.45.35. Listing of the top 100 French firms along with key personnel in each company.**

XI. APPENDIX

A. SAMPLE CURRICULA VITAE

Charlotte Jones Dubois
15, avenue Napoléon
75016 Paris

Tel: 45.98.76.77

* 12 ANS D'EXPERIENCE EN COMPTABILITE

* BILINGUE - FRANCAIS / ANGLAIS

FORMATION

9/80 - 6/82 **M.B.A.**	Columbia University School of Business New York, N.Y. (Option: Comptabilité)
9/75 - 6/79 **B.A.**	University of California, Los Angeles, Calif. (U.C.L.A.) Bac + 4 (Option: Economie)

EXPERIENCE PROFESSIONNELLE

11/86 à ce jour   **Contrôleur de Gestion**   Pechiney, Ugine, Kuhlmann, Paris, France

     *Gestion de 5 filiales: plan de financement, comptabilité analytique, comptabilité générale, gestion budgétaire et fiscalité.

7/82 - 9/86   **Chef Comptable**   Pechiney, Ugine, Kuhlmann, Greenwich, Conn. Etats-Unis

     *Comptabilité générale, enregistrement du bilan 1983-85, déclarations fiscales et sociales pour 3 filiales.
     * Comptabilité analytique.

10/79 - 6/82   **Analyste de Gestion**   Bank of America, Los Angeles, Californie, Etats-Unis

     *Chargée du reporting mensuel du chiffre d'affaires.
     *Préparation du budget annuel.

7/79 - 9/79   **Assistant Analyste**   Bureau des Statistiques, Los Angeles, Californie, Etats-Unis

     *Chargée d'analyser les budgets des départements.

LANGUES

Français/Anglais: bilingue
Espagnol: lu, écrit

INFORMATIQUE

IBM, Apple
Software: Lotus 123, D Base III, R Base

DIVERS

Nationalité:	Américaine, Carte de Séjour, Permis de Travail
Age:	34 ans

B. Chronological; mixture of professional and volunteer experiences

Louise Johnson Bourgeois
59, rue Bonaparte
75006 Paris

Tel: 49.57.87.45

EXPERIENCE ACQUISE
*Direction de programmes, activités et promotions.
*Direction de séances d'ergothérapie.
*Editeur de livres sur des sujets divers.
*Professeur d'anglais

EXPERIENCE

9/91 à ce jour   Directrice, Département des Langues, ABC Traductions, Noisy le Grand

2/90 - 8/91   Vice-Présidente, Programmes, Association d'Accueil des Etrangers

         *Organisation des activités mensuelles pour l'association
         *Rédaction d'un manuel d'instruction pour tous les membres
         du conseil d'administration

2/90 - 10/90   Editeur de *Writers Writing in Paris* pour l'association "Letters and Words" (groupe réunissant de jeunes écrivains à Paris)

         *Un guide en anglais sur tout ce que les écrivains doivent savoir pour être publié

1/86 - 3/89   Présidente de "Letters and Words", Paris

         *Edition de 35 dépliants sur divers sujets
         *Edition de 4 lettres d'information par an
         *Organisation de grandes fêtes et tombolas
         *Promotion de l'association pour en assurer la croissance
         *Création de services gratuits pour les membres

9/85 - 1/86   Vice-Présidente de "Letters and Words", Paris

         *Edition du livre *Letters and Words Cookbook for Busy Writers* (le livre de
         cuisine des écrivains très occupés)

1/85 - 6/88   Professeur d'Anglais, Institut de Gestion Sociale, Paris

         *Enseignement tous niveaux pour adultes
         *Rédaction de leçons pour cours par minitel
         *Enseignement par téléphone

3/82 - 4/84   Professeur d'Anglais, Institut de Langues Vivantes, Paris

         *Enseignement tous niveaux pour adultes
         *Responsable de l'intégration des nouvelles méthodes d'enseignement pour leur
         diffusion auprès des autres professeurs

1/79 - 8/81	<u>Ergothérapeute</u> (Recreational therapist),Ellis Hospital, Syracuse, New York (USA)

        *Organisation des activitiés pour les malades mentaux
        *Thérapie du sport et de l'art
        *Direction de séances de thérapie de groupes
        *Participation aux réunions avec les médecins et psychologues pour décider de la meilleure approche envers chaque patient

1/79 - 8/80	<u>Directrice des Programmes</u>, Military YMCA, Miami, Florida (USA)

        *Organisation des activités pour les Marines
        *Discours de présentation dans les bases militaires
        *Responsable des relations publiques concernant les activités

FORMATION

9/74 - 6/78	<u>Kenyon College</u>, Gambier, Ohio (USA) Psychology (Maîtrise en Psychologie, Bac + 4)

LANGUES

Bilingue (Français - Anglais)

NATIONALITE

Americaine (Carte de séjour, Carte de Travail)

Julie B. PICARD
4, rue Jean Moulin
75017 Paris
Tel: 45.97.08.43

M.B.A. FINANCE: Master's Degree in Business Administration, (Maîtrise de Gestion)
BILINGUE: Français/Anglais
OBJECTIF: Gestion Financière

EXPERIENCE PROFESSIONNELLE

Finance

* Elaboration du système d'analyse des investissements pour une société de fabrication de produits électroménagers.
* Analyse financière d'une société d'équipements automobiles.
* Evaluation et analyse boursière sur le court et moyen terme d'une société métallurgique.

Management/Gestion

* Elaboration d'un projet traitant de l'amélioration de la gestion des risques dans les institutions bancaires.
* Gérant d'un magasin de chaussures (chiffre d'affaires mensuel moyen: 725.000FF, personnel: 5)

Informatique

* Bonne maîtrise IBM PC et Macintosh
* Très bonne connaissance de Lotus 123, Excel

FORMATION

M.B.A.   <u>University of Chicago</u>, Chicago, Illinois (USA), 1984 - 1986

B.A.   <u>University of Southern California</u>, Los Angeles, Calif. (USA) 1980 - 1984
(Option: Economie)

DIVERS

Date de Naissance: 24 juillet 1962
Nationalité: Française/Américaine
Langues: Bilingue: Français/Anglais
Notions: Allemand, Espagnol

Annette Lewis Chardon
29, square Beaulieu
75016 Paris

Tel: 43.59.69.01

EXPERTISE EN GESTION DES RESSOURCES HUMAINES

RECRUTEMENT   Définition et analyse des postes
Recherche de candidats internes et externes
Sélection des lettres de candidature
Travail avec les sociétés d'intérimaires

SYSTEMES D'EVALUATION
Mise en place des systèmes d'évaluation pour ouvriers, employés et techniciens
Préparation différentes filières des plans de carrières
Evaluation des systèmes de formation

REMUNERATION ET PAIE
Connaissance des systèmes de paie, charges sociales et assurances
Connaissances des textes législatifs et de la jurisprudence concernant les
problèmes de rémunération

EXPERIENCE

1986 - 1991   Directrice Adjointe - Ressources Humaines
Colgate Palmolive, Paris, France

1981 - 1985   Directeur du Recrutement
Honeywell Bull, Paris, France

1976 - 1980   Responsable Rémunérations
Honeywell Corporation, San Francisco, Calif. (USA)

ETUDES

1975   Certificat en Administration du Personnel
University of Wisconsin, Madison, Wisconsin (USA)

1972   B.A. (Licence)
Mount Holyoke College, Massachusetts (USA)
(Option: Français)

LANGUES   Français-Anglais: Bilingue

DIVERS   Née: USA 30 juin 1950; mariée; permis de travail

B. SAMPLE COVER LETTERS

Sample Cover Letter A   *to be handwritten*

Mlle Sylvie Bourge
25, rue Angélique
75011 Paris

Paris, le 21 avril 19XX

Directeur du Personnel
IBM Europe
Tour Pascal-la-Défense
22, route de la Demie
92834 Puteaux

Votre référence: 599

Monsieur,

Suite à votre annonce du 20 avril, parue dans "Le Figaro", je vous prie de trouver ci-joint mon dossier de candidature pour le poste d'Assistante Administrative chez IBM Europe.

Parfaitement bilingue Français-Anglais, je suis fortement motivée et intéressée par ce poste. J'ai le sens de l'organisation et des contacts.

Convaincue d'être en mesure de vous apporter une collaboration efficace, je souhaiterais vivement vous rencontrer. Je serais heureuse de vous donner plus de détails au cours d'un entretien.

Dans cette attente, je vous prie de croire, Monsieur le Directeur, à mes sentiments distingués.

(signature)

Sylvie Bourge

P.J. Curriculum Vitae

Sample Cover Letter B   *to be handwritten*

Paris, le 15 octobre 19XX

Mme Rosemary Dupré
4, allée des Fernes
92420 Vaucresson

Amway France
14, avenue Franz Liszt
92164 Antony Cedex

Monsieur,

Votre annonce parue dans "Le Monde" sous la référence T O38 227 a retenu toute mon attention.

Le profil de la personne recherchée ainsi que la description de ses futures activités m'engagent à vous soumettre ma candidature.

Avant de m'installer à Paris, j'ai travaillé dix ans dans un département commercial. J'ai de bonnes connaissances de gestion, comptabilité et administration. De nationalité britannique, je parle couramment le français, ayant passé plusieurs années en France.

Dans l'attente de pouvoir vous rencontrer, je vous prie d'agréer, Monsieur, l'expression de mes sentiments respectueux.

(signature)

Rosemary Dupré

<u>**Cover Letter C**</u>   <u>*to be handwritten*</u>

Paris, le 9 février 19XX

Paul Herbert
364, rue de Vaugirard
75015 Paris

REF: F 90 45 678

Madame, Monsieur,

Suite à votre annonce parue dans "Le Monde" du 8 février, je me permets de solliciter l'emploi de chef du Personnel au sein de votre entreprise.

Ma formation universitaire juridique, en licence puis en maîtrise, m'a permis d'acquérir les connaissances nécessaires pour prétendre exercer cet emploi.

Dynamique, motivé dans mon travail, organisé et sociable, je souhaite devenir le responsable du personnel que vous recherchez.

Je me tiens à votre disposition afin de vous rencontrer et de vous fournir les renseignements dont vous souhaiteriez disposer.

Je vous prie de croire, Madame, Monsieur, à l'assurance de ma considération distinguée.

(signature)
Paul Herbert

DIVORCE IN FRANCE

by

Carla K. Potok

Avocat à la Cour

and

Persis Gouirand
Ellen Grandsard
Judy Stewart-Vidal

editing by Alexandra Boutin

Divorce in France

ABOUT THE AUTHORS

Born in the United States, AAWE member **Carla Kewley Potok** received her undergraduate degree from a small, private college before doing graduate work at the University of Washington in Seattle. In 1976, she came to France, married a Frenchman and graduated from the Paris University Law School with Honors. She is currently a French lawyer.

She has worked as personal assistant to a former First President of the French Supreme Court on international arbitration questions before entering a large French-American law firm where she did legal consulting before moving on to an important French litigation firm. She was appointed as a Fellow by the Twenty-first Century Trust, an English trust created by several ambassadors to the UN early in the 1980s to promote democratic values in the world. In addition to AAWE, she is an active member of the American Chamber of Commerce in Paris. She lectures on comparative French-American law questions.

She has now set up her own law practice and developped an important clientèle in different fields of international private law such as inheritance, labor law, divorce and international child-custody.

ABOUT THE EDITOR

Alexandra Boutin grew up in Washington, D.C. and graduated from Vassar College. She is a freelance writer and editor whose work is published regularly in FRANCE TODAY. Several of her essays will soon appear in an anthology on the international life entitled CROSSING BORDERS. She is currently working on a book about life in France. A long-time member of AAWE and co-editor of the AAWE Guide to Education, she is the mother of three children.

ABOUT THE CONTRIBUTORS

Persis Gouirand, a graduate of Wheaton College in Massachusetts, received her Masters from the Middlebury College Graduate School of French in France. She is married to Jean-Pierre Gouirand and is the mother of three children.

Having lived in France for twenty-five years, she is now a partner with two other AAWE members of At Home Abroad, an executive relocation company whose business is introducing other foreigners to Paris.

Persis joined AAWE in 1978 and has volunteered her skills in various capacities including several years as editor of the AAWE newsletter.

Ellen Grandsard, psychologist and mother of four children, joined AAWE in 1969. She is a graduate of Wellesley College and the University of Paris (D.E.S.S. in Clinical Psychology). Trained in the U.S. and Europe as a family therapist and mediator, she has worked for over fifteen years with adults and children in private practice and on the staffs of the CHU (hospital) of Beaumont-sur-Oise and Pontoise. Member of the American Association of Family Mediators, the French *Association pour la Promotion de Médiation Familiale* and the European Association of Family Therapy, Ellen has a private practice in Paris.

Judy Stewart-Vidal joined AAWE in 1987. She is a graduate of Barnard College with a degree in Political Science. In France, she became involved in the theater as a director and producer. She agreed to undertake this section on divorce at the inception of the project. Her ideas provided the outline for this section of the <u>AAWE Living in France</u>.

DIVORCE IN FRANCE

Section 1: The Legal and Financial Aspects of Divorce by Carla K. Potok

Section 2: Divorce Mediation by Ellen Grandsard

Section 3: Personal Commentaries on Divorce (Introduction by Judy Stewart-Vidal)

Section 4: Useful Addresses and Resources edited by Persis Gouirand

Section 1: THE LEGAL AND FINANCIAL ASPECTS OF DIVORCE

by Carla K. Potok, *Avocat à la Cour*

Table of Contents

V. PROTECTIVE MEASURES FOR PROPERTY

VI. LEGAL SEPARATION (*Séparation de Corps*)

VII. LEGAL AID (*Aide Judiciaire*)

VIII. FILING A CLAIM AGAINST A BELLIGERENT SPOUSE

IX. REMARRIAGE and *Délai de Viduité*

X. APPLICABLE LAW AND JURISDICTION

XI. CHOOSING A LAWYER AND FEES

XII: CHARTS: Schematic Summary of Divorce Procedures and Their Respective
        Consequences

I. FRENCH DIVORCE LAW

1.1. INTRODUCTION

From a legal point of view, divorce is like a freeway: if you take the wrong ramp, you must continue in the wrong direction for quite some time without being able to make a U-turn and often do not reach the proper destination. It is therefore essential to study the map of divorce before venturing onto the freeway. I am going to try and help you study that map before departure.

By this analogy, I mean that it is very difficult for couples who have already begun divorce proceedings to realize that a divorce cannot -- and should not -- only be considered as a short-term solution to a crisis situation. Divorce is a long-term commitment. Its emotional and financial consequences will influence the future of spouses and children for years to come. In short, divorce is something which must be planned.

There are two main stages to a divorce: living THROUGH the divorce and living WITH the divorce.

To understand why I insist on this issue, one must step back from the present crisis situation which has made divorce seem inevitable and decide what should be derived from a divorce in order for life to remain tolerable both for the spouses and for their children, from an emotional as well as a financial point of view.

This brief guide will attempt to direct you through the initial stages of divorce and help you see what is on the other side of the tunnel. The type of divorce chosen will be largely determined by the results required in order for each spouse to start a new life and for the lives of the children to continue with minimal change and damage.

To better understand current French divorce procedures, it is useful to take a quick look at the origins of divorce in France.

Before the Napoleonic Civil Code of 1804, the influence of the Catholic Church was such that marriage was considered eternal and not subject to dissolution. Adultery was the only exception to this rule. In order to circumvent the rigid religious view of divorce, courts often simply annulled marriages.

The French Revolution of 1789 brought a breath of fresh air by allowing divorce on grounds of incompatibility or by mutual consent. However, this liberalism led to extremes which caused Napoleon I to seriously clamp down on divorce. A series of divorce laws were codified in 1804. It is important to briefly look at this Civil Code because divorce in France was defined by this system from 1804 to 1975 -- therefore, until quite recently.

The major characteristic of divorce under Napoleon was that it was considered an offense not only against one's spouse but also against society. In other words, divorce was thought of, literally, as a criminal offense for which the "guilty" spouse should be punished and the "innocent" spouse indemnified by payment of damages. Divorce for fault predominated. One could divorce for three reasons: adultery (the "hot bed" case which will be explained further on), brutality and belligerent behavior (*sévices et injures graves*), or affront to the reputation of one's family, in cases where a spouse had received a criminal sentence.

The Napoleonic definition of adultery was that of the "hot bed case". The innocent spouse usually hired a private detective who would come early in the morning and feel the sheets to see whether they were hot on both sides of the bed. In most cases, such proof was very difficult to obtain. However, adultery could also be proved by testimonies.

This rigid system led to the admission of divorce for "brutality and injurious behavior", which generally boiled down to adultery without "hot bed" proof. The "guilty" spouse could not be caught red-handed. This second cause also covered belligerent behavior and physical violence.

The third cause is self-explanatory. Divorce could be filed by the "innocent" spouse of an individual sentenced to prison for a crime or fined for a misdemeanor: Napoleon felt that the spouse, who had already been socially punished because of the offense committed by his or her spouse, suffered, in addition, the humiliation and slanderous effect of any adulterous behavior of which the other party was equally guilty and should, therefore, have the right to divorce.

Divorce by mutual consent did not exist.

Guardianship of the children depended upon who had committed the "fault", since the "innocent" spouse usually was judged more trustworthy.

The "guilty" spouse could be condemned to pay the "innocent" spouse a kind of alimony, which covered not only the material needs of the "innocent" spouse, but also damages caused by the "guilty" spouse's behavior.

Legal separation existed in 1804 (*séparation de corps*). The grounds for legal separation were the same as those for divorce with the exception that, in the case of legal separation, the spouses had to remain faithful to each other throughout the separation.

The absence of mutual consent as a means of divorce led to couples staging their divorce by what was called the *divorce-comédie*. Spouses who agreed to divorce were more or less obliged to pretend one was the "guilty" party and produce testimonies to that effect.

Slowly it became obvious that this system was no longer adapted to modern society, especially following the sexual revolution of the 1960's -- the advent of the pill, legalized abortion, women's lib. Also, divorce had become more socially acceptable. The idea of divorce by mutual consent gained ground, based on a single criterion: when marital life became intolerable, divorce appeared to be the only remedy. Divorce as punishment inflicted upon an unfaithful spouse no longer seemed adequate. Since the spouses could now choose how to organize their divorce, the idea that divorce could become contractual emerged.

There were two major reasons for the divorce reforms of 1975: the legal procedure no longer reflected accepted standards of behavior, and the criminal repercussions were getting out of hand. Public figures could easily find themselves blackmailed and manipulated by spouses in a divorce for fault, leading to criminal investigation and scandal.

The legislators in 1975 had a great deal of difficulty conciliating the notion of fault and divorce as punishment, which had originated in the religious morals of the Napoleonic era, with the new acceptance of divorce and sexual liberty.

Our present-day divorce law is a compromise between the original causes for divorce, as defined in the Napoleonic law -- divorce for fault (*faute* per se, or *rupture de la vie commune*) and divorce for objective reasons (mutual consent upon joint petition or divorce by mutual consent requested by one spouse and accepted by the other, although this latter form of divorce usually leads to a shared fault divorce as explained below).

In the divorce proceedings which entail the fault of one's spouse, the judge arbitrates the spouses' dispute and dirty laundry gets washed in court.

In the case of mutual consent, the judge has a passive role. Both parties direct the proceedings and finalize a divorce contract. Family laundry is washed in private, and the judge only sees the final product -- the divorce contract -- to which he may or may not give legal force.

In any case, the major criterion is the unbearable nature of marital ties (*le caractère intolerable du maintien de la vie conjugale*).

Since 1975, all divorce cases have been handled by highly specialized judges called *juges des affaires matrimoniales* (or J.A.M.).

1.2. CHOICES OF DIVORCE PROCEEDINGS

There are currently four types of divorce in France:

-divorce by mutual consent (*consentement mutuel* or *sur requête conjointe*)

-divorce by mutual consent but requested by one party and accepted by the other (*demande acceptée par un époux à la requête de l'autre*, otherwise known as *demande acceptée*),

-divorce for fault (*faute*),

-divorce for disruption of cohabitation (*rupture de la vie commune*).

a. MUTUAL CONSENT UPON JOINT PETITION (*requête conjointe*)

Many couples today choose divorce by mutual consent. This type of divorce, however, is not always a possibility. Certain conditions must be fulfilled: the spouses must have been married for more than six months; they must agree to the divorce; they must agree on HOW to divorce; they must agree on the consequences of the divorce and especially how the divorce will affect the spouses, their children, and the joint estate; the spouses must remain in agreement throughout divorce proceedings.

Divorce by mutual consent is the least expensive form of divorce. One lawyer will sometimes suffice for both parties. However, if negotiations prove too difficult, the parties may choose to hire two lawyers which doubles the cost of legal fees. The services of a *notaire* are but limited to drawing up the legal document which evaluates joint property, necessary for the liquidation of that property. The *notaire* does not arbitrate differences of opinion.

Divorce by mutual consent is also the fastest kind of divorce. The procedure is simplified.

Finally, divorce by mutual consent is more discreet. Dirty laundry gets washed at home. Not even the judge knows the reasons which have caused the couple to appear before him.

The judge must attempt to reconcile the two parties. Both spouses will be requested to meet with the judge and present a tentative divorce contract which will remain valid throughout the divorce proceedings.

Following this first hearing, there is a compulsory period during which the spouses are asked to think over their decision. The J.A.M. sets the duration of this period, legally from three to nine months.

During this period, the spouses present a final divorce contract to the judge who may or may not give it legal force. This contract provides for child custody and visiting rights, for alimony in the sense of child support (*pension alimentaire des enfants*), for *prestation compensatoire* (a French term for which there is no American equivalent -- see II. Child Support and Alimony for the meaning of this term), and finally, for allocation of the family lodging and distribution of joint property.

The judge will ask the spouses to reiterate their mutual consent. If the spouses do so, the judge must pronounce the divorce and only has the right to rectify any major financial imbalance.

This procedure doesn't have only advantages. There are several disadvantages. One is the precariousness of the spouses' agreement. In case of disagreement, the divorce proceedings are declared invalid, as if the spouses had never decided to seek a divorce in the first place. In order to divorce following such disagreement, the spouses must file for divorce a second time.

In certain cases, a divorce by mutual consent may be used by one spouse to entrap the other. An example would be when, under the impression that the agreement is total, one spouse decides to live with his/her mistress or lover. The other spouse may attempt to use this behavior to transform the mutual consent form of divorce into divorce for fault by using testimonies of adulterous behavior.

b. MUTUAL CONSENT (*demande acceptée*)

The second type of divorce is called divorce by mutual consent requested by one spouse and accepted by the other (*demande acceptée*). This form of divorce is a hybrid of divorce by mutual consent and divorce for fault. Judges have a tendency to decide there is shared fault. Couples consent to the divorce at different intervals. One spouse files for divorce by sending his/her spouse a written report, or *mémoire*, explaining why maintaining marital life has become intolerable and listing the reasons for divorce. The law states that this report should be objectively written.

(1) Submission of the *mémoire*

Upon receipt of this report, the receiving spouse has one month to either accept or refuse it. If the receiving spouse accepts the report of the requesting spouse, there is mutual consent, deferred in time. Such acceptance shall be manifested by the receiving spouse's written version of the facts as seen from his/her point of view, in response to the requesting spouse's report. The judge will establish that the two spouses have confessed (*double aveu*).

(2) Reconciliation attempt

The judge will then order the spouses to court in an attempt to get them to reconcile (*audience de conciliation*). After this hearing, the judge will issue a court order called a *procès-verbal de non-conciliation* in which she/he will declare reconciliation impossible. The judge will also declare that the spouses have mutually agreed to divorce and that they accept the reasons for divorce. This is the point at which the court establishes that there has been a *double aveu*.

(3) Designation of a *notaire* and child custody investigation

The judge may designate a *notaire* to proceed with evaluation of joint property. He/she will also hear proposals on custody of the couple's children. Following this first hearing, the judge will set further dates for carrying out the practical aspects of the divorce itself.

As soon as the judge has established that the spouses have mutually confessed to and accepted the report of the other spouse, the principle of being able to divorce is definitively and irrevocably acquired. Should one of the spouses change his or her mind, it is too late.

Another particularity of *demande acceptée* is that, should the spouses not be able to agree on practical and financial matters, the court will decide for them, contrary to divorce upon *requête conjointe*. A *notaire* will be designated to evaluate joint property. He/she will execute the court order and liquidate the joint estate.

One advantage of *demande acceptée* is that, since the court and the *notaire* are in charge of the liquidation of the joint estate and the execution of any court order concerning custody of children, family disputes are somewhat limited. This type of divorce also avoids delays in the liquidation of joint property since a time schedule for liquidation is established by the court.

However, there are also multiple disadvantages to *demande acceptée*. The procedure is considerably longer. It is much more expensive since it requires the services of two lawyers and one *notaire*. It is also less discreet since the spouses resolve their differences in court rather than in private. The spouses are less free to choose the consequences of their divorce, as the judge and the *notaire* will, in most cases, do that for them. Should such intervention not be necessary, there would be no need for this form of divorce, and the spouses would file instead for divorce by mutual consent (*requête conjointe*).

It should be noted that, if the spouses have filed for divorce by mutual consent but cannot agree on a divorce settlement, they may transform the divorce by mutual consent into a divorce by *demande acceptée*. It must be emphasized that this form of divorce does not allow the spouses to negotiate on financial matters. The court will decide for them on the basis of equity, and in the best interest of the children.

It is important to understand that, contrary to American law, French law does not seek to maintain the previous standard of living for both partners. The French judge will ONLY attempt to give the financially disadvantaged spouse the possibility of getting on his/her feet and starting a new life. **Therefore, the idea of being able to maintain one's standard of living after a divorce must be abandoned.** This is not generally the French judge's aim. In practice, however, French courts have a tendency to be more lenient without this being compulsory. (We will examine this topic as it relates to the financial consequences of divorce in greater detail as we proceed.)

The court has jurisdiction to issue a divorce decree but not to liquidate property. Only a *notaire* can liquidate property. If the spouses disagree on the *notaire*'s evaluation, the judge will arbitrate.

c. DIVORCE FOR FAULT

Divorce for fault still exists in contemporary France, but the notion of fault is extremely subjective and can be interpreted in different ways. The judge can take into consideration the social situation of the spouses, their religious morals, race, or any other factors which might have an influence on the spouses background and education. The law itself is very vague. Today's definition of fault is "serious behavior rendering the continuation of marital life intolerable" (*motif grave et sérieux, rendant intolerable le maintien de la vie commune*), a much broader definition than that established by the Napoleonic Code. Divorce for fault today may include adultery, criminal sentence, belligerent or violent behavior, etc.

Should one spouse decide to file for divorce for fault against the other spouse, a local lawyer should be consulted, since only local lawyers are truly familiar with what their local courts consider as fault.

For example, in an interesting case which took place within the community of authors and actors, one spouse decided to file for divorce for fault. The requesting spouse was a notorious playboy. One evening, he showed up with his mistress at a posh party on the Riviera. Unfortunately, his wife was at the same party and saw her husband walk in with another woman. The humiliated wife decided to get even on the spot and released her shoulder straps so that her dress dropped to the ground. She stood there, stark naked, in front of all the celebrities, then jumped into the swimming pool. The husband attempted to use this incident to prove that his wife's unacceptable behavior was rendering marital life impossible.

The local courts did not agree with his interpretation. They considered that the wife's conduct was not as scandalous as the husband maintained: the actors and authors present had all either participated in nude scenes in movies or had written similar scenes into their novels. Therefore, the court pronounced divorce "for shared fault", not for fault against the woman.

This example illustrates the importance of the "milieu". Had the woman done the same thing at a formal dinner, given by well-known aristocrats in a private chateau, it is not at all clear whether the court would have made the same decision. The judgment might also have been different had the woman behaved in this manner during some religious festival.

In a divorce for fault, one spouse files for divorce for fault against the other and produces affidavits and testimonies to support or prove faulty behavior.

If one of the spouses refuses to divorce, then the judge has the right to search for elements which would permit him/her to pronounce the divorce against the will of the other spouse. The judge can even attribute half of the fault to this spouse.

In cases where one spouse obtains a divorce for fault against the other, the financial consequences can be considerably more onerous for the "guilty" spouse, as we will see further on.

d. DIVORCE FOR DISRUPTION OF COHABITATION

The fourth type of divorce is called divorce for "disruption of cohabitation" (*rupture de la vie commune*). This divorce is usually used when everything else has failed.

There are certain conditions prerequisite to filing for divorce for *rupture de la vie commune*: the couple must have been separated for at least six years, one of the spouses' mental faculties may have been severely altered for a period of six years, and "community of life" is no longer possible. Should this type of divorce be granted, the spouse who files will be held responsible. He/she will generally be charged with desertion. He/she will be deemed the "guilty" spouse, as it were. This *répudiation* or "penalty" divorce penalizes the spouse who has abandoned the marital home for more than six years.

In a *rupture de la vie commune* divorce, the spouse charged with the fault for divorcing must pay heavily. When this type of divorce is requested, the judge must pronounce the divorce. The defendant can refuse to divorce and attempt to use what is called the *clause d'exceptionnelle dureté* or hardship clause.

The *clause d'exceptionnelle dureté* means the defendant tries to convince the judge that such a divorce would have material and moral effects of extreme hardship on him - or herself - and the children. In such a case, the judge may refuse to grant the divorce. The judge is entirely free in his/her interpretation of the notion of *exceptionnelle dureté*. Therefore, the definition is based on case law and is highly subjective.

An example of *exceptionnelle dureté* would be if a woman in her sixties were to lose her social position following a divorce. Another example would be if a person who is seriously ill risked losing access to French health insurance (*Sécurité Sociale*). The fact that divorce is an intolerable concept for religious people would also be a valid reason.

In a case of *exceptionnelle dureté*, the judge may either refuse to grant the divorce or pronounce the divorce and put the entire blame on the requesting spouse. The financial consequences for the requesting spouse will be considerable since, in this type of divorce, the duty to aid one's spouse (*devoir de secours*) remains. The requesting spouse may have to pay not only alimony, but also damages.

This form of divorce is quite rare, considering the strict conditions under which it applies.

It does NOT apply if the spouses have not been separated for more than six years, or if the mental faculties of one of the spouses have not been altered for the previous six years, rendering "community of life" intolerable.

In addition, the filing spouse who earns a decent living should avoid this type of divorce and choose rather divorce for fault, due to the dire financial consequences.

1.3. CONCLUSION

It is essential to consult a lawyer as early as possible when the "community of life" gets difficult or intolerable.

Divorce for fault is a solution to a crisis situation, whereas mutual consent is a remedy to an intolerable marriage.

Mutual consent is the only form of divorce which allows the spouses to divorce and liquidate their own property from the very beginning.

The financial consequences of divorce must be examined from two different points of view: the consequences for the children and the consequences for the spouses.

II. CHILD SUPPORT AND ALIMONY

When a spouse refuses to contribute financially to the family's needs, whether or not the spouses live separately, the negligent spouse may be ordered by the Tribunal d'Instance to contribute to such needs. However, such contribution ceases when divorce proceedings begin.

During divorce proceedings, you will be hearing two terms which are very distinct and have different financial implications:

-*prestation compensatoire*, a French form of compensation which has no real equivalent under American law, and

-*pension alimentaire*, which is closer to the American notion of alimony or "maintenance".

Each one of these two forms of compensation has its own particular raison d'être. They should not be confused.

2.1. Compensation for children

The divorce decree will establish custody. Whatever the cause of divorce, the decree will require that the parent to whom custody of the children has NOT been given continue to contribute to the child's education and maintenance (*à l'éducation et à l'entretien de l'enfant*). The amount due will vary in function of the child's needs (health, interests, education) and the respective financial situations of the parents. Child support is a form of *pension alimentaire*.

When the court establishes the amount of compensation which the non-custodial parent should contribute monthly, the sum is not definitively and irrevocably acquired. It is subject to annual variation according to the cost of living index. This is a rule of French public order.

Each parent will be asked to contribute to the child's needs as his or her resources permit, not only until the child becomes of age, but also until the end of the child's studies. This form of alimony can be maintained during professional training periods after the child has completed his/her studies. In some cases, based on a recent decision by the French Supreme Court, the period can extend until the child has landed his first paying job.

2.2. Compensation for spouses

Compensation must be considered in two stages: compensation during the divorce proceedings, or *pension alimentaire*, which is closer to the American notion of alimony, and compensation after the divorce, or *prestation compensatoire*, which has no real equivalent under American law.

a. Compensation during divorce proceedings

Spouses have a duty to aid one another after filing for divorce and until divorce is pronounced (*devoir de secours*, provided for by Article 212 of the French Civil Code). This obligation takes the form of alimony in the sense that the more privileged spouse gives the less privileged spouse enough money on which to live. However, there is absolutely no notion of damages, unlike under American law.

In all forms of divorce except *rupture de la vie commune*, this form of compensation ceases with the definitive divorce decree.

The opposite is true for *rupture de la vie commune*: the "duty to aid" obligation is maintained for the spouse who has abandoned "community of life" after the divorce is pronounced.

The criteria for setting the amount of compensation are the same as for the *pension alimentaire* for the children. The spouses' respective financial needs and revenues are taken into consideration. Under French law, however, if a woman works, it is sometimes difficult for her to obtain a *pension alimentaire* during divorce proceedings despite major discrepancies between her revenue and that of her spouse. This is unfortunate and unfair, but it is the current trend.

If the spouses do not agree on the sums fixed by the court, they may appeal the temporary *pension alimentaire* before a Court of Appeals. Such a request is called an appeal against the writ of non-conciliation.

It is also important to emphasize here that the *pension alimentaire*, or "alimony", paid throughout the divorce proceedings ceases to exist once the divorce becomes final. After the divorce, "alimony" as understood under American law, takes the form of *prestation compensatoire*, without the notion of damages.

b. Compensation after divorce

Once a divorce is pronounced, the spouses' obligation to mutually help each other out ceases.

The *prestation compensatoire* is set by the court and takes into consideration the respective economic situations of the spouses and their respective estates and personal property, including joint property, personal property, any undivided property, and future "hopes" for income.

After divorce, the notion of differences in the standard of living disappears and is replaced by the criterion of substantial disparity (*disparité substantiel*). The spouse who suffers from the "disparity" may ask for a *prestation compensatoire*. Unlike alimony and *pension alimentaire*, this *prestation compensatoire* serves to correct the difference between the two spouses' standards of living for a certain period of time (determined after the court's evaluation of the respective financial situations).

The *prestation compensatoire* is supposed to enable the spouse suffering from the disparity to begin a new life. Its function or purpose is NOT to re-establish a balance between the financial situations of the two parties or to maintain the standard of living of the victimized spouse after the divorce, as is the case in the United States. The *prestation compensatoire* only serves to give the disadvantaged spouse a breath of fresh air, enabling him/her to get back on his/her feet and fulfill his/her own financial needs.

For instance, a man making a good living as a senior executive in a big French firm was married to a woman who possessed real estate assets but did not have a profession. The wife attempted to use the fact that she had no profession to obtain a large *prestation compensatoire* from her husband, who was a salaried employee. The French Court of Appeals took the woman's assets into consideration and decided she should benefit from a monthly *prestation compensatoire* for only three months.

It is very important to understand that, prior to 1975, under French law, the notion of *pension alimentaire* was linked to the life span of the spouse receiving support. The opposite is true for *prestation compensatoire*: payment is not necessarily linked to the life span of the spouses. It can be limited in time and even reduced at a given time, for example upon the retirement of the paying spouse.

The judge may also opt for a *prestation compensatoire* without any limitation in time. If this happens, the time frame is bound to the life span of the person who receives it, which can lead to bizarre complications. For example, an elderly man divorced his first wife who had three children. The court decided that this gentleman would pay his first wife a monthly *prestation compensatoire* without limiting the payment of this sum in time. This gentleman later married a much younger woman and had two more children. He then died. The deceased man's obligation to pay a monthly *prestation compensatoire* to his first wife was passed on to his heirs. As a result, the second wife was required to pay the first wife a monthly *prestation compensatoire* despite the fact that she had two small children and was no longer being supported by her husband. Modification of a *prestation compensatoire* is possible only in exceptional cases. Therefore this woman could not even request that the court change the amount in view of her altered revenues.

In cases where the spouses decide to divorce by mutual consent, the monthly *prestation compensatoire* may be deemed a forfeit, not subject to revision. It is, however, possible to insert a revision clause into the final divorce contract.

The law sets forth very exceptional cases in which the *prestation compensatoire* can be revised.

It is important to note that even in the case where the paying spouse loses his or her job, the *prestation compensatoire* cannot be modified.

The *prestation compensatoire* can also be settled as a lump sum of capital, paid in cash. In this case, the paying spouse is supposed to be able to provide the total amount in one single payment.

It should be noted that the courts take the length of the marriage into consideration when they determine how much *prestation compensatoire* someone should receive. A spouse married only two or three years would not be awarded the same amount or length of payment as a spouse divorcing after twenty-five years of marriage.

The notion of financial consequences of divorce is highly complicated by an element on which the French Supreme Court has not yet clearly stated its position: the revenues of the *concubin(e)* can be considered when determining the amount of the *prestation compensatoire*. The judge may request information concerning the spouses' revenues, as well as those of their respective lover or mistress. This is where the notion of "hopes of income" come into the picture. The question submitted to the French Supreme Court is whether or not the judge can fix the amount of *prestation compensatoire* owed by one spouse to the other according to the receiving spouse's hopes not only to inherit from his/her family, but also to benefit from the income of his/her *concubin(e)*. Certain courts have gone so far as to review the accounts of the companion. Other courts have followed suit. The French Supreme Court has not yet taken a position on this issue.

It should be noted that this is proof that the notion of fault, as understood during the Napoleonic era, has almost totally disappeared, since some courts are beginning to take the social position of the *concubin(e)* into consideration in order to determine the financial consequences of a divorce. One court granted child custody to a mother who lived with her well-to-do companion -- another way of forgiving the mother's fault and of punishing the innocent husband, who did not have custody and might have preferred that his child live in the family home, rather than with the *concubin*. A judge may even request that the *concubin(e)* be heard. This situation is truly a perverse effect of the law. The French Supreme Court will undoubtedly be called upon, in the near future, to take a firm stand on whether such hearings will be permitted or not.

The moral of all this is that living with someone during divorce proceedings may prejudice the financial outcome of the divorce for the "guilty" spouse.

It should be noted that, prior to the reform of 1975, the Civil Code provided for *pension alimentaire* which included what we now call the *prestation compensatoire*, on the one hand, and damages paid by the "guilty" spouse, on the other. Payment usually was no longer due on the death of one or the other of the spouses. How different things are now!

Prestation compensatoire as we know it now boils down to a redistribution of the joint estate at the time of its liquidation and can be fixed in favor of one of the spouses rather than on the basis of a fifty-fifty division, which should normally be the case if the spouses are married under the legal regime of the *communauté reduite aux acquêts*.

If the *prestation compensatoire* is to be settled in capital, it may be paid at the time of the liquidation of the estate. For example, let's imagine that the divorcing couple has joint ownership of an apartment. Should the woman wish to continue to live in the apartment, she may be requested, during liquidation proceedings, to pay a certain amount in capital as the counterpart for her husband's ownership. In this event, the woman would have full ownership of the apartment at the outcome of the divorce. The husband would be compensated by an amount equal to the value of his share in the apartment (called a *soulte*).

It should be kept in mind that the liquidation of the marital estate and the notion of *prestation compensatoire* are inseparable.

It is impossible to determine the form of divorce for which the spouses should file without analyzing their estate (or absence thereof).

The *prestation compensatoire* requested during divorce proceedings is going to heavily influence the liquidation of joint property after divorce.

The financial hopes of the spouses AND the financial situation of the *concubin(e)* may be taken into consideration when the amount of *prestation compensatoire* is being set. If the *concubin* is a taxi cab driver, no risk is involved. However, if the *concubin* is a rich banker, it is wiser not to live together until after the divorce has been granted.

In current divorce proceedings, the moral element has seriously diminished, paving the way for an increase in the financial importance of divorce.

Here I would like to give an example which will illustrate how the hopes for a *prestation compensatoire* can be changed by circumstance:

A woman with breast cancer was abandoned by her husband. The husband ran off with his secretary. Divorce was pronounced for fault. An expert was appointed by the court to evaluate the amount of *prestation compensatoire* which should be allocated to the wife. The husband appealed the decision. Between the moment when the lower court rendered its verdict on the divorce and the moment when the Court of Appeals ruled on the appeal, the situation changed: the woman's father died and she inherited his estate. The Court of Appeals took this new element into consideration when finalizing the amount of *prestation compensatoire* to which she was entitled.

Prestation compensatoire, paid monthly, is tax deductible. The paying spouse deducts it from his taxes and, therefore, generally pays less in taxes than before. The receiving spouse, however, declares the *prestation compensatoire* as additional income, which often increases the taxes. If the *prestation compensatoire* is paid in capital, it is tax-free.

In the case of division of joint property, the *droit d'enregistrement* (registration fee) is only one percent of the total value of the property. However, when the spouses are married under the *régime de la séparation des biens* (marriage contract by which each spouse maintains ownership of personal property acquired before marriage), any undivided property is subject to the payment of real estate transfer fees at the time of the division and will be taxed as a transfer of property, including capital gains, at ten percent. In this case, the spouses may estimate the value of their property as they wish without the intervention of a *notaire*. In general, the French tax authorities do not challenge this sort of transfer because estimates are usually reasonable. However, in the case of resale, capital gains will be heavily taxed, with the exception of the principal dwelling.

III. PAYMENT AND RECOVERY OF COMPENSATION (for both *pension alimentaire* and *prestation compensatoire*)

3.1. Payment

a. Installments

Compensation is generally paid in twelve monthly installments and should be paid in advance. Vacation costs for spouses who take their children on vacation do not affect or reduce compensation payments in any way. They constitute additional out-of-pocket expenses incurred by the spouse paying compensation. For example, Ginette and Albert are divorced. Ginette has child custody, and Albert pays child support every month. Albert decides to take the children on vacation in August and pays for their food and lodging during this period. He still owes child support to Ginette for the month of August.

b. Cost of living adjustments (*indexation*)

When *prestation compensatoire* is paid monthly, adjustment for the cost of living is automatic.

The *pension alimentaire* is not automatically adjusted. You may request its adjustment from the court and propose the applicable price index. (The monthly consumer price index is the one most frequently used. Others exist, however. Variations can be obtained from the INSEE -- *Institut National de la Statistique et des Etudes Economiques* -- by writing or phoning the local INSEE office, or by consulting the minitel 36-15 or 36-16 Code INSEE.)

3.2. Recovery of unpaid compensation

a. Recovery of compensation in France

If your ex-spouse does not pay, does not regularly pay, or only partially pays compensation, you have several options:

1) direct payment (*paiement direct*);

2) retainer placed on the ex-spouse's salary (*saisie-arrêt sur salaire*);

3) seizure of the ex-spouse's personal effects (*saisie-exécution*);

4) recovery through the Treasury Department

5) In addition, as an advance on child support, under certain conditions, you may be entitled to receive a pension called an *allocation de soutien familial*.

1) *Paiement direct* enables you to recover compensation without filing a new claim before the court. As soon as the paying spouse fails to pay compensation as it falls due and, if you have been awarded compensation by a court order which has become enforceable, you may be paid directly by the paying spouse's employer or banking institution (*banque, centre de chèques postaux, caisse d'épargne*, etc.). To obtain payment, simply notify the employer or banking institution of your request to benefit from this direct payment procedure through a *huissier de justice*, competent for the place of your residence. Send the court order which awarded you compensation (*pension alimentaire* or *prestation compensatoire*) along with information on the paying spouse, such as his/her identity and address, *Sécurité Sociale* number, bank account number, and employer's address.

Further, the following organizations possess information concerning the paying spouse's financial status and are obliged to provide your *huissier* with the data you request. They are, among others, the Tax Authorities, *la Sécurité Sociale*, national bank account data banks, and data banks for *cartes grises* (registration of personal cars with departmental authorities). The organization concerned is notified by registered letter with return receipt requested. The *huissier* informs the paying spouse at the same time.

This procedure allows for the recovery of the following: compensation as it falls due and any unpaid compensation due during the six months prior to the notification of the direct payment procedure. The latter will be payable in equal installments over a twelve-month period. Unpaid compensation in excess of this six-month period may be recovered through other procedures and, in particular, by *saisie-arrêt sur salaire* and *saisie-exécution*.

2) *Saisie-arrêt sur salaire* allows you to be paid by the paying spouse's employer, as in the case of *paiement direct*, but by court order. The court which has jurisdiction is the *Tribunal d'Instance* located in the place of the paying spouse's residence (or *arrondissement* for Paris). You are not required to be assisted by a lawyer, but you may ask a lawyer, a *huissier*, or any other person of your choice to represent you before this court, provided such a person has a mandate.

3) *Saisie-exécution* allows you to have the paying spouse's movable personal property (car, furniture, appliances, etc.) seized and auctioned in order to obtain the recovery of compensation on the proceeds of the sale.

4) Recovery through the French Treasury Department is a last resort: If the first three procedures have failed, you can ask the Treasury Department for help. To do so, send a registered letter with return receipt requested to the French equivalent of the American district attorney (*Procureur de la République*) of the *Tribunal de Grande Instance*, having jurisdiction

over the locality of your place of residence. You must include the following information with your request:

- the court order which has awarded compensation,

- any documents which establish that recovery could not be obtained through the other procedures (an affidavit from the court bailiff in case of, for example, direct payment),

- any information you possess about the paying spouse (name, address, profession, *Sécurité Sociale* number, bank account numbers, employer's address).

This method of recovery concerns compensation as it falls due and future compensation, as well as those sums which remained unpaid over a period of six months prior to the date of the request for recovery by the Treasury Department; this provision allows the Treasury to recover its costs. Such costs result in an increase in the sums to recover and will be incurred by the paying spouse, as well as any other expenses, such as legal fees, etc.

5) You may be eligible to receive an *allocation de soutien familial* as an advance on child support if the following three conditions are met:

- your children are your dependents, making you eligible to receive *prestations familiales*;

- if you can produce a court order awarding you child support;

- you live alone (ie. you do not live with anyone and have not remarried).

This pension amounted to 429 FF as of January 1, 1992. In order to receive it, you must go to the *Caisse d'Allocations Familiales* closest to your place of residence or to the office which normally pays your *prestations familiales*. Your local *Caisse d'Allocations Familiales* can also be requested to recover any compensation due by an ex-spouse.

b. Recovery of compensation abroad

Recovery of compensation abroad is more problematic. As a general rule, if you are confronted with this problem and if you live in France, you should contact the *Procureur de la République* (French equivalent to a district attorney) of the *Tribunal de Grande Instance* of the locality in which you live. If you live outside France, you should contact either the Ministry of Justice or the Ministry of Foreign Affairs of the country in which you live, or the local French consulate.

3.3. Modification of the amount of compensation due

Exceptionally, you can request revision of the *pension alimentaire* and, in limited cases, of the *prestation compensatoire* when your financial needs or resources have significantly changed since the last court order.

This would be true if you are receiving insufficient compensation and wish to request an increase. If you are paying compensation and can no longer assume payment due to retirement, accident, illness, or loss of employment, you can also request that the court reduce the compensation or even, in certain cases of extreme necessity, eliminate it entirely. It should be emphasized that if you seek a reduction, it is in your interest to do so as soon as possible since you remain responsible for compensation due (plus interest) for as long as the amount you pay has not been officially revised by court order.

As a general rule, the judge who has jurisdiction is the *J.A.M.* of the locality where the spouse, not having initiated revision proceedings, lives. Requests for revision may be filed either by sending a letter to the *J.A.M.* or by filing a claim through a lawyer.

3.4. Recourse against refusal to pay compensation

There are two cases in which refusal to pay compensation is considered a criminal offense, punishable by prison and fine: *abandon de famille* and *changement de domicile*.

a. Desertion of family (*abandon de famille*)

When the paying spouse has not paid the entire amount of either the *pension alimentaire* or the *prestation compensatoire* due, you can file suit for desertion of family. To do so, write a letter to the *Procureur de la République* having jurisdiction either over the locality in which you live or over the locality in which your ex-spouse (the paying spouse) lives.

Filing a claim for *abandon de famille* does not constitute a remedy for recovery of compensation but a form of criminal pursuit which can be a means of putting pressure on a spouse who obstinately refuses to pay.

Furthermore, the spouse condemned for *abandon de famille* loses his/her right to parental authority over the children and, in particular, loses visiting rights for as long as she/he has not begun to carry out his/her obligation to pay and has not done so for six months.

b. Change of residence (*changement de domicile*)

After divorce or legal separation, any spouse who has an obligation to pay a *pension alimentaire* or a *prestation compensatoire* and does not notify his/her ex-spouse of any change of address may be sentenced to prison or fined.

IV. CHILD CUSTODY

4.1. French rules on custody

In approximately sixty percent of French divorce cases, the court decides that child custody should be granted to the mother. In the remaining forty percent, the judge decides fifty percent custody for the husband and fifty percent for the wife. The legal criterion for custody is the best interests of the child. The judge tries to find a solution which will put an end to any family dispute on this matter as soon as possible.

Since the 1987 reform of French law, the judge can no longer automatically give full powers to decide for the children to only one parent. Prior to 1987, custody of children was granted to one or the other of the parents and, as a general rule, to the mother. In 1987, with the evolution of the role of the father within the family structure, the legislator made it possible for both parents to have "joint" custody over the children (*autorité parentale conjointe*).

What actually changed for divorcing parents? Since 1987, the judge examines what custody situation will best protect the interests of the children who come first under the new law. If he feels that it is in the children's best interests to be under the authority of only one of the parents, he can grant authority to that one parent but must establish, and thereby protect, the other parent's visiting rights.

As a general rule, the parent not having authority is granted the right to visit his/her children. Visiting rights take two different legal forms: *droit de visite* and *droit d'hébergement.*

The *droit de visite* applies to weekends. This often allows the non-custodial parent to see his/her children the first and third weekend of every month from the end of school on Friday until Sunday night at 8 p.m.

The *droit d'hébergement* applies to school holidays. Often this right allows the children to live with the parent not having custody for half of all school holidays. In this case, the children often spend half of the short holidays (*Toussaint*, Christmas, February holiday, Easter) and half of the long holidays (summer vacation) with one parent and half with the other. (This means, for example, half of August is spent with one parent and the other half of August with the other parent.)

Visiting rights may be established subject to the presence of a third party or subject to visits being conducted in a specific place, following a social worker's inquiry as to the children's psychological balance and welfare.

Sometimes the judge feels that the better interests of the children warrant his granting joint authority (not to use the word "custody"...). This is a more flexible system: the divorced parents decide together on their children's future, and the judge only decides where the children will live as a general rule. The children may, in fact, have two homes. Visiting rights are often established so as to avoid eventual conflict in case of disagreement. Joint authority is usually granted when the parents' relationship appears good enough to convince the judge that the children will not be used as instruments to settle differences. Court-ordered visiting rights such as those explained above apply only when the couple cannot reach agreement. If joint authority is granted, the parents and the judge must decide where the children will spend their leisure time, which parent will benefit from the tax deduction created by the children's presence, which parent will be responsible for the children's acts, and how much support the other spouse will contribute to help the parent living with the children to cover their costs.

Furthermore, since 1987, the judge has been required to ask children over age 13 with whom they prefer to live. This interview is optional for younger children. Before 1987, children had no voice in the matter.

4.2. Social worker's investigation (*Enquête sociale*)

Before deciding upon child custody, whether temporary or final, and upon visiting rights, the judge may order that an *enquête sociale* be carried out by a qualified person whom she/he designates. This person is usually a social worker. He/she will collect information on the family situation both from a material (housing, material needs) and a moral (child abuse, violence, family relations) point of view . The investigation will attempt to establish the general conditions under which the children live and are raised. However, the investigators must scrupulously respect the privacy of the family under investigation.

The social worker will determine which measures should be taken to best protect the children's interests.

By definition, such an investigation is ordered against one of the parents. This parent cannot present his/her defense. Therefore, the parent who is the object of the inquiry may request that the judge order a counter investigation (*contre-enquête*). Such a counter investigation does not, however, have any effect on the one-sided nature of the initial inquiry whose findings are either completed or contradicted.

At the end of the investigation, the social worker will submit a report to the court.

The cost of the investigation may be incurred by one or both of the parents. The judge will solve this issue in the decision by which he orders the investigation and fixes the amount to be prepaid in order for the investigation to get under way.

During the inquiry, the social worker may find factual information which is pertinent to divorce proceedings (adultery, suspicious behavior ...). Such information may not be used in the legal discussion of the causes for divorce, given the unilateral nature of the social worker's inquiry.

4.3. French rules on taking children abroad

As a general rule, your children cannot leave France without your authorization. However, in conflictual situations, for instance before or during divorce or separation, attempts may be made to take your children out of France against your will. There are preventive measures which may be taken in this case. These differ according to whether or not you have filed for divorce or legal separation, as explained below.

Here is a situation which may present itself if you are married and have not yet filed for divorce/legal separation: Throughout the marriage, the two parents have had joint authority over the children. One or the other parent may authorize the children to travel abroad. For example, either parent may possess a passport established in the children's names or have the children's names put on his/her own passport.

If your spouse wants to take your children abroad against your will, there are administrative measures which can be taken so that the children cannot cross the border.

When children travel abroad without one of their parents, they must have a special card bearing their picture and the signature of one parent (*autorisation de sortie du territoire*), valid for one year.

If this is the case for your children, you may officially protest such authorization by filing what is called an *opposition à sortie du territoire*. To do so, go to the passport office of the *préfecture* in the locality where you live. Take your *livret de famille*. In case of emergency, and, in particular, at times when the *préfectures* are closed, go to the nearest police station, then regularize the procedure at the *préfecture* the first day it is open thereafter. You must do so within a period of seven days.

This temporary measure is only valid for fifteen days. In order to prolong its effects, you may request what is called an *interdiction de sortie du territoire* which prohibits the children from leaving France. To obtain it, file a request with the *juge des tutelles* of the *Tribunal d'Instance* nearest your home (or, for Paris, within your *arrondissement*). This procedure is free and does not require the assistance of a lawyer.

Once you have obtained this court order, send it to your *préfecture*, which will distribute it to the appropriate offices at the Ministry of the Interior, as well as to customs and border police. Be sure to indicate not only the children's identities, but also the identity of the person(s) who may attempt to take the children abroad. The prohibition is valid for one year but may be renewed, if you so request, by your *préfecture*. Absolute effectiveness cannot be guaranteed given the volume of transit between neighboring countries.

Now we will examine the case where you are divorced or divorcing and the *J.A.M.* has granted you parental authority over the children and has established your ex-spouse's visiting rights. You fear that your ex-spouse will take advantage of his/her visiting rights to take your children abroad. When you file for divorce, request that visiting rights be limited to French territory. As mentioned previously, you may also request that the judge specify where the visits will take place. This implies that the parent not having custody can only see the children in a place established by the judge, your house, for example, or the house of someone in whom you have confidence, or a center operated by a specialized non-profit organization, such as an *association d'accueil*.

If you agree that your children may be taken abroad by your ex-spouse but want to take precautionary measures, you may request that the court declare that visiting rights which entail removing your children from France be subject to certain conditions such as prior recognition of the French custody decision by foreign authorities.

V. PROTECTIVE MEASURES FOR PROPERTY

The law of 1975 which reformed divorce in France provides for recourse against the spouse who attempts to fraudulently dispose of joint property once divorce has been filed.

Under French law, any obligation entered into by one of the spouses concerning property which belongs to the joint nuptial estate, any transfer of joint property, following the date on which divorce was filed, by one of the spouses within the limits of his/her power to transfer, will be declared null and void if there is evidence that the deal was concluded with a view to swindle the other spouse.

This rule applies only to joint property and only where one spouse's rights to such property are in jeopardy. It excludes prejudice suffered by any third parties.

However, this provision is only rarely applied by the courts for unexplained and unexplainable reasons.

In addition to this specific rule related to divorcing couples, the law provides for various other more general recourses which may be applied in cases of divorce. The judge has the power to take any foreseeable measures to forbid a spouse from endangering the family's interests. The judge may also declare null and void acts performed fraudulently in violation of conservative measures taken to preserve family interests. This applies to any type of nuptial agreement.

Couples who married under the legal *régime* of the *communauté légale réduite aux acquêts*, which prevails in the absence of a specific nuptial agreement, are affected by three additional legal stipulations: One spouse may act in place of the other spouse in certain cases to make decisions the latter would normally make himself; each spouse may file a claim against the other in order to prevent him/her from allowing personal property to go to waste or to be squandered or misappropriated and, in particular, to protect the revenues generated by such property; one spouse may request that the court declare null and void any acts entered into by the other spouse in violation of his/her right to decide about joint property.

The general trend in French law and case law seems to be towards increased protective measures for each spouse. This change will lead to increased protection for women who are often at a disadvantage since men usually manage family affairs.

VI. LEGAL SEPARATION

Couples unsure of whether or not to seek a divorce may want to consider legal separation as a "wait and see" strategy. Either spouse may file a petition asking the court to declare the spouses legally separated, to authorize them to live separately, and to set forth the financial consequences of such a separation.

The spouse against whom divorce is filed may answer by filing for a legal separation. Inversely, the spouse against whom a request for judicial separation has been filed may file for divorce. If both a request for separation and a request for divorce are filed simultaneously, the court will pronounce a divorce on the grounds of shared fault.

The causes for legal separation are the same as those for divorce: mutual consent upon joint petition, mutual consent requested by one and accepted by the other, fault, and disruption of cohabitation for more than six years.

The proceedings for a legal separation follow the same general rules as for a divorce.

In the case of a legal separation, the marriage is not dissolved: the marriage link is only weakened. The obligation for the married couple to live together ceases. **However, the couple are still obliged to remain faithful, making adultery dangerous business since anyone who lives with a companion during this period risks seeing his/her behavior used as evidence in a divorce for fault.**

Spouses who married under the *régime de la communauté réduite aux acquêts* fall under the *régime de la séparation des biens* once they have been legally separated.

The "duty to aid" (*devoir de secours*) subsists throughout a judicial separation. A *pension alimentaire* will be due. However, there will not be any *prestation compensatoire* since this form of compensation is attributed only AFTER a divorce.

At the end of three years of separation by mutual consent (either by joint petition or by *demande acceptée)*, if both spouses still agree, the judicial separation can be transformed into a divorce by mutual consent.

After three years of a separation for fault or for disruption of cohabitation, if one of the spouses wishes to divorce, the divorce will be automatically declared and cannot be challenged.

If one spouse is caught committing adultery during the period of legal separation, that spouse loses the right to claim a *prestation compensatoire* once divorce is pronounced.

The *pension alimentaire* will vary according to the spouses' financial situations and will be set by the court.

If the measures established by the court (custody, *pension alimentaire*, visiting rights, etc.) seem to suit all parties, they are often maintained in the divorce decree. Legal separation may serve as a testing ground for a future divorce.

It should be noted that one can be accused of *abandon de domicile* **if 1) one leaves the conjugal domicile before filing for legal separation, or 2) before obtaining the court's authorization to live separately once a divorce has been requested.**

VII. LEGAL AID (*Aide Judiciaire*)

7.1. Who may benefit from legal aid

Foreigners whose residence is habitually France, as well as French citizens, are eligible for legal aid. Such aid may be total or partial, according to the beneficiary's income.

Full legal aid (100%) is provided for persons whose annual income for the preceding year (January 1 to December 31) was less than 3,465 FF (ceiling established as of publication of the present guide, subject to periodic revision), excluding social family pensions (*prestations familiales*).

Partial legal aid (i.e. not 100%) is provided when the beneficiary's average monthly income, excluding *prestations familiales*, is less than 5,250 FF and the assistance of a lawyer is required (divorce, for example). If the assistance of a lawyer in not required (problems concerning rent, for example), that sum falls to 4,225 FF.

These ceilings are increased by 390 francs per dependant. Dependants are defined as any person under 18 years of age (25 years for students), without any age limit for disabled or handicapped persons, spouses without personal income, or dependant parents whose income is less than the minimum pension allocated to elderly persons (*minimum vieillesse*).

7.2. How to apply for legal aid

The legal aid office, or *Bureau d'Aide Judiciaire*, is located in the same building as the *Tribunal de Grande Instance*. This office distributes application forms as well as lists of documents to submit with the application. The legal aid office informs each applicant of its decisions on an individual basis.

7.3. Emergency legal aid

Temporary emergency legal aid may be requested by persons who have been subpoenaed before the court for an upcoming hearing, or where legal proceedings are already under way.

7.4. Consequences of legal aid

The beneficiary is entitled to the services of both a lawyer and all legal personnel required. Legal aid beneficiaries may freely choose their lawyer if they find a lawyer who is willing to accept their case. However, since lawyers receive virtually no compensation for legal aid cases, often they refuse.

If you are eligible for legal aid but do not know any lawyers, or, if those you contact will not represent you, a lawyer will be appointed by the *Bâtonnier*. (The *Bâtonnier* is a lawyer elected by fellow attorneys to represent the Bar; she/he is responsible for imposing disciplinary measures upon the other lawyers of his Bar.) Lawyers appointed by the *Bâtonnier* are not necessarily specialized in the type of law you need. For example, if you seek a divorce, you will not necessarily be assigned a "divorce" lawyer.

Should you receive full legal aid, you will not have to pay any legal fees.

Should you receive partial legal aid, you will be required to pay only a nominal lump sum, fixed by the legal aid office in proportion to your income.

7.5. Additional expenses following the court's decision

If you lose your case and are ordered to pay court costs, you will be liable for expenses incurred by your adversary as a result of the proceedings, unless the court decides otherwise.

If you win your case, your lawyer may, under certain conditions and with the *Bâtonnier*'s approval, bill you for extra fees when the court award provides an amount sufficient to cover them.

In any case, you will be liable to the French Treasury Department for the reimbursement of any outstanding taxes or costs incurred for acts or titles you produced during the proceedings. These expenses are generally minor and may be related to legal formalities, such as registration fees.

7.6. Income ceilings limiting right to benefit from legal aid

Number of Dependents	Full Legal Aid if salary does not exceed:	Partial Legal Aid: when a lawyer is NOT required and income does not exceed:	Partial Legal Aid: when a lawyer is required and salary does not exceed:
0	3,465FF/month	4,225FF/month	5,250FF/month
1	3,855FF	4,615FF	5,640FF
2	4,245FF	5,005FF	6,030FF
3	4,635FF	5,395FF	6,420FF
4	5,025FF	5,785FF	6,810FF
5	5,415FF	6,175FF	7,200FF

VIII. FILING A CLAIM AGAINST A BELLIGERENT SPOUSE

Victims of violence often feel ashamed and keep the abuse a secret. Their fear of escalation and social criticism often prevents them from seeking help.

It is important for victims to realize that such cases are much more common than one realizes and that they exist at all socio-economic levels. There is nothing shameful about being a victim of abuse. One should not be afraid of bringing it out in the open.

The only way out of this kind of situation is to seek help. It is important to obtain written traces of the violence through medical certificates, x-rays, filing claims, etc. Without written evidence, a legal remedy cannot be found. Proof of violent acts must be obtained immediately following such an act in order to have full judicial weight in court. Otherwise, the court cannot prove the cause-effect link which is necessary to sentence the aggressor.

Battered spouses should, therefore, immediately file a claim against the violent spouse on the grounds of *coups et blessures*.

Battered spouses should also seek medical attention as soon as possible. If the abuse occurs at night, one can go to the emergency ward of a nearby hospital in order to obtain a medical certificate, x-rays, etc. as proof of the violence.

It is important to know that claims should not be filed against a given individual but against "X", i.e. an unidentified person. The reason for this is to protect victims from a slander lawsuit (*diffamation*) should the violent spouse be acquitted and attempt to take revenge through a slander claim. Under French law, there are 3 ways of filing a claim (*déposer une plainte contre X*):

1.) You can file a report at the local police station (*Commissariat de Police*).

2.) You can send a letter to the *Procureur de la République* of the local *Tribunal de Grande Instance* (located at the *Palais de Justice* for Paris residents).

3.) You can file a claim with the *Doyen des Juges d'Instruction*.

In the first case, a claim is filed with the *Commissariat de Police* nearest the location where the offense took place or closest to the domicile of the person who committed the offense. There will be either a police investigation or the police will decide the offense is not serious enough to warrant investigation. Depending on the results of the investigation, the police may transfer the file to the District Attorney, or *Procureur de la République*, for legal action.

In the second case, a letter is sent to the *Procureur de la République* of the *Tribunal de Grande Instance*. The *Procureur* will weigh whether or not it is in the Public's interests to pursue the offender. If the decision is favorable, he will transfer the file to the *Doyen des Juges d'Instruction* who will assign a specialized judge, called a *Juge d'Instruction*, to the case. This judge has more power than the police. If the *Procureur* decides not to take legal action, the claim will be filed without action at this level.

These proceedings do not require a lawyer and are free of legal costs, but they tend to be very drawn-out and only lead to legal action in cases of serious offenses which endanger public safety. Indeed, the police officer or *Procureur* decides unilaterally if there is sufficient evidence to indict the offender or not.

The third possibility is to file a claim directly with the *Doyen des Juges d'Instruction*. While this may be done without the assistance of a lawyer, it is advisable to seek assistance here in order to ensure that court proceedings are followed properly. If the *Doyen des Juges d'Instruction* feels the offense is serious enough to warrant legal action, he will assign a *Juge d'Instruction* straightaway to investigate the case.

The *Juge d'Instruction* has extensive investigative powers and can order protective measures where necessary.

While this third procedure saves time and may increase your chances of bringing the claim to court by short-circuiting the police services and the *Procureur*, you must expect to pay attorney's fees for filing, and then for pleading, should the case be brought to court.

You will be asked to pay an advance on court costs, or *consignation*, which will be refunded once the offender is convicted since she/he will be required to pay all costs, in addition to damages.

IX. REMARRIAGE AND *DELAI DE VIDUITE*

I would like to draw your attention to the following requirement under French law which, in practice, does not pose a major problem: in order to avoid problems related to paternity, a woman's remarriage is subject to certain conditions and, as a general rule, to her remaining single for a three-hundred day period called the *délai de viduité*.

In a divorce for disruption of cohabitation, this stipulation does not apply since, by definition, this form of divorce implies that the woman has not been living with her ex-husband for more than six years. There is, therefore, little danger of her not being able to determine whether or not her ex-husband is the father of a child she may be carrying. However, in all the other forms of divorce, a woman must abstain from remarrying for three hundred days. The starting point for this period differs according to the form of divorce chosen:

In a divorce by *requête conjointe*, the interim starts on the day when the judge gave legal force (*homologation*) to the temporary divorce contract (*convention temporaire*), following the initial hearing.

In a divorce by *demande acceptée*, it is the date of the initial hearing that counts.

In a divorce for fault, the waiting period begins on the day when the judge issues a decision stating that the couple cannot reconcile their differences or that they plan to live apart.

This interim period automatically expires if the woman has a baby following the date set forth above or if she produces a medical certificate stating that she is not pregnant.

X. APPLICABLE LAW AND JURISDICTION

As a general rule, French law applies to the divorce or legal separation of all couples whose principal residence is on French soil. This policy applies even when both spouses are foreigners.

The court having jurisdiction is that located nearest the family home. If the spouses live separately, jurisdiction is given to the court of the place in which the children live.

However, conflict may arise when one spouse is French and the other is foreign, and their joint residence is abroad, as French divorce law does not offer a specific solution to such cases.

A problem is also created when the spouses, French and foreign, live in two different countries.

Theoretically, the French spouse can attempt to impose French jurisdiction on the foreign spouse by application of the French rule of exclusive jurisdiction (articles 14 and 15 of the Civil Code) under which any French citizen, wherever he or she may reside, has the right to be heard by a French judge before a French court.

For example, Judith, an American citizen, married Maurice, a French citizen, in California. They then came to France where they bought property together, set up a household, and had children. Once the children were grown, the relationship deteriorated. Judith finally decided to return to the United States. She filed for divorce in California since they had been married there.

Maurice continued to live in the family house in France where all joint property was located.

Upon receiving service of process from a California divorce court, Maurice immediately filed for divorce in France on the basis of his right to be heard by a French judge.

Meanwhile, in California, the American judge declared that he had jurisdiction over the divorce and issued a divorce decree, with the understanding that the French judge had not yet issued a divorce decree in France. However, the American judge declared that he did not have jurisdiction over the liquidation of joint property since it was located in France.

Confusion ensued. Maurice attempted to impose French jurisdiction by pretending that the American judge had refused to issue a divorce decree and providing the French court with an inaccurate translation of the American decision.

In retaliation, Judith immediately requested that the French judge give legal force to her American divorce decree in order to have it carried out in France -- such a procedure is called exequatur. She asked the French court to agree that it did not have jurisdiction to issue a second divorce decree in spite of the French exclusive jurisdiction rule, explained above.

To make a long story short, Judith finally managed to get her ex-husband to withdraw his French divorce claim by producing a correct translation of the American decision showing that the American court did have jurisdiction and had issued a divorce decree prior to the French court. She also had evidence that her ex-husband had implicitly accepted the jurisdiction of American courts by never having contested the American proceedings. Consequently, he could no longer benefit from the exclusive jurisdiction rule.

I mention this example to show that this exclusive jurisdiction rule is systematically applied by French judges except where a French citizen has expressly waived his/her right to benefit from it.

In Judith's case, divorce proceedings, of course, took a long time due to this conflict over jurisdiction, which was the result of the French spouse's deliberately seeking French jurisdiction in bad faith since he knew that his ex-wife had already filed for divorce in the United States.

Furthermore, while the American court was finally accepted as having resolved the divorce question, liquidation of joint property was carried out by the French court and *notaire*.

In order to avoid expensive and lengthy legal proceedings such as those endured by Judith, it is preferable to consult a lawyer who can foresee conflicts, both abroad and in France, and attempt to avoid them prior to your filing for divorce.

XI. CHOOSING A LAWYER

American citizens, and more generally any foreigners living in France, have a more complex choice to make when choosing a lawyer than do French nationals. In addition to general criteria such as competence, affinities, and fees, Americans need to consider a lawyer's capacity to:

-understand international legal questions and solve eventual conflict of law issues which may arise ,

- converse in English when explaining French law questions,

- correspond in English with a foreign lawyer when both French and foreign courts are involved.

costly and time-INEFFICIENT and should be avoided.

The following explanation of criteria may be considered when making your choice. Its purpose is to inform you on the organization of the legal profession in France, requirements for competence, and fee structure.

1. COMPETENCE AND SPECIALIZATION

a) General competence

In France, the legal profession is highly controlled by the *Conseil de l'Ordre*. It controls access to the legal profession in order to guarantee consumers quality legal services offered by competent individuals having the required professional training. Sanctions are inflicted upon individuals who violate such requirements.

In 1991, new legislation was imposed on the legal professions and the professions of *avocat* and *conseil juridique* merged. Before 1991, *avocats* were traditionally litigation lawyers while *conseils juridiques* did not have the right to plead before all courts and generally only did consulting. The new law abolished this distinction. In addition, it attempts to increase the protection of consumers against "legal impostors" who give legal opinions to unwary clients without having the proper training. While controls have become more strict, there are still numerous "impostors". Please be cautious of people offering legal services at reduced rates. You could be the victim of their incompetence in case of a lawsuit. Qualified lawyers are registered on one of the French bars and are subject to control by the *Conseil de l'Ordre*.

b) Specialization in French law

In France, as in the United States, law is divided into two main fields: private, or civil law, and corporate law (*droit des affaires*). Basically, civil law concerns individuals and families whereas corporate law concerns companies. It is difficult to be highly qualified in both, given the wide spectrum of legal issues. Within each of these fields, there are many sub-specializations, one of which is divorce.

Therefore, the first question to ask is: do I need a *civiliste* (civil law specialist) or an *avocat d'affaires* (corporate lawyer). Once this question has been answered, a certain guarantee of quality is assured. A good *civiliste* will usually be qualified to handle any civil law issue, one of which is divorce. A good corporate lawyer is trained to handle corporate law questions.

In France, it is not always easy to determine a lawyer's specialization. French lawyers have only a very limited right to advertise. Recently, they have been granted permission to distribute a brief promotional brochure on their activities to clients. However, the *Conseils de l'Ordre* has a computer listing of lawyers and their specializations which may be consulted by the general public.

For the Paris Bar, this listing is located in the offices of the *Conseil de l'Ordre des Avocats* at :

Palais de Justice
4, boulevard du Palais
75001 Paris

Go to the front desk *(Accueil)* which faces Stairway A.
Hours: 9-12h and 14-18h; except Friday, 17h.

In the greater Paris area, there are major Bars located in Nanterre, Bobigny, and Créteil. Each one has its own Hall of Justice and *Conseil de l'Ordre*.

Although a good source of information, this listing is not exhaustive since all qualified lawyers may not have registered by their specialization.

c) Further specialization in international and EEC law

Americans living abroad often encounter international or bi-cultural issues which need to be solved within the context of what appears, at first glance, to be a purely French-French legal problem. It may become essential (and be cost-efficient) to consult an international law specialist from the outset. The following are a few examples of difficulties which may arise:

- The American party does not understand complex French legal jargon and requires the assistance of a bilingual lawyer.

- The dispute may entail lawsuits pending simultaneously before both French and American courts.

- In some cases, rules governing conflicts of law (a field of international law) may take precedent over local law.

It may be necessary to obtain, through the French courts, the right to proceed in France with the execution of a decision ordered by an American court.

In divorce, there are often elements requiring an international law specialist such as: liquidation of property both in France and in the U.S.; recovery of unpaid alimony from the French spouse living in France by the other spouse who may live in the U.S.; problems of child custody when parents live on two different continents, including recovery of children unduly taken abroad by one spouse.

These issues may be further complicated by liquidation of property owned in several EEC countries. International law and EEC law are additional specializations which Americans living abroad should consider in their choice.

The American Embassy can provide a list of lawyers who practice in France and have experience in the resolution of international law disputes. American organizations in Paris may be able to help you to find someone qualified to handle your situation. Another source would be the American community in Paris; friends and family may be able to recommend a lawyer based on first-hand knowledge of his/her performance.

2. PERSONAL AFFINITIES

Often lawyers cannot take the time to explain what is going on. Being confronted with legal proceedings in one's own country creates stress. Being confronted with legal proceedings in a foreign country where you do not know the legal system and may not even speak the language may be emotionally difficult. Part of a lawyer's role is to humanize the judicial machine. She/he should also serve as an intermediary between the client and the French Administration as a whole (police, judges, etc.)

It is essential to be able to communicate with your lawyer, to have the confidence that she/he will explain what is happening, keep you informed, and defend your interests as aggressively as may be necessary.

You have a right to be informed about important elements in your case. However, this does not imply that your lawyer can and should spend hours explaining procedural details to you.

3. FEES

To understand why fees often seem a delicate subject for discussion in France, we must take a brief look at historical taboos linked to lawyers and fees before the French Revolution of 1789.

Prior to 1789, lawyers and court judges were traditionally nobles who lived in castles and managed family estates. They practiced law in their spare time on a pro bono basis. Power and fortune were closely linked. Justice was in the hands of rich nobles. Often common people were subjected to unjust court orders, torture, high taxes or capital punishment.

The Revolution abolished this justice system. Napoleon rewrote the laws. (The actual *Code Civil* dates from 1804). However, the pre-revolutionary legal system had a strong influence on the post-revolutionary period.

Immediately following the Revolution, lawyers were no longer trusted and were suspected of disloyal conduct. A new breed of lawyers emerged. Power, wealth and justice separated. The new lawyers worked independently of financial and political concerns. As a result, many lawyers feel ethically inhibited from revealing their need for compensation. They pretend the fee question is not a major issue and avoid it completely, yet bill just the same. This attitude, of course, leads to confusion, especially on the part of American clients.

In France, lawyers' fees are indirectly controlled by the *Conseil de l'Ordre*. The American fee structure of "contingency fees" or "no win, no fees" is prohibited in litigation cases. This measure intends to prevent French lawyers from earning the colossal sums American lawyers have the reputation of demanding.

These cultural and historical differences can be a source of misunderstanding which I hope the following explanation will help to alleviate.

a) Fee structure established by the *Conseil de l'Ordre*

1. Calculation of fees

Fees are generally set in consideration of:

- the work carried out,

- the difficulty of the case,

- the lawyer's notoriety and specialization,

- the operating costs of the lawyer's firm,

- the significance of the interests concerned.

2. Billing and *Conventions d'Honoraires*

Lawyers generally make every attempt to foresee costs and fees so as to inform clients. However, this is not always possible.

It is advisable to sign a *convention d'honoraires* which is a contract between the client and the lawyer establishing a means of calculating fees and providing for billing dates.

Fees may be hourly or based on a lump sum where it is possible to determine such sum. Only exceptionally are they determined by a given result, as explained below.

When fees are based on the actual number of hours spent working on the case by the lawyer, the hourly billing rate and Value Added Tax should be specified in the *convention*. The V.A.T. should also be specified for lump sum fees.

When the legal services rendered do not concern litigation, fees may be calculated <u>only</u> upon results obtained or services rendered. Such results should be explicitly defined in the *convention* as well as the percentage applied, the lump sum due, and the time at which it shall be considered that a result has been obtained.

When there is litigation, fees cannot be calculated solely on the results of the lawsuit. They will first be calculated on the services rendered. A *convention* stating that additional fees will be due, based on the result of the hearings, may also be drawn up.

When there is no *convention*, fees are generally considered due on an hourly basis.

Lawyers will systematically ask the client to pay a retainer (*provision*). It is against this retainer that fees and costs due will be charged.

When the case comes to a close, the lawyer sends a final bill.

b) Disputes

In the event a dispute arises over payment of fees, the *Bâtonnier* will arbitrate. He will either grant the lawyer the right to pursue his client before the court for recovery of fees or he may reduce them if he feels they are too high. A reduction, though, has to be amply justified. The *Bâtonnier*'s decision is subject to appeal.

If the *Bâtonnier* grants the lawyer the right to pursue a client for recovery, all ordinary legal means of recovery apply as would be the case for the recovery of any debt.

XII: CHARTS: Schematic Summary of Divorce Procedures and Their Respective Consequences

Chart 1: Comparative Chart of the Four Divorce Procedures

A. Mutual consent by joint petition or *consentement mutuel*
B. Mutual consent to divorce, filed by one spouse and accepted by the other or *demande acceptée*
C. Divorce for rupture of cohabitation or *rupture de la vie commune*
D. Divorce for fault or *faute*

Type of Divorce	1. BASIC CONCEPT	2. TYPE OF PROCEDURE	3. JURISDICTION	4. TERRITORY COMPETENCE
A. Mutual Consent, Joint Petition (*consentement mutuel*)	Prior mutual consent of the spouses	No dispute situation (couple agrees on everything)	Judge assigned to matrimonial cases (J.A.M.)*	If living sep-arately:choice between place of residence of one or the other spouse ; if cohabitation:place of joint residence
B. Mutual Consent, deferred in time (*demande acceptée*)	Mutual consent which is deferred in time based upon statement of the facts by one spouse, later accepted by the other spouse	Dispute situation	J.A.M.: for pre-litigation and declaration of divorce Court: for consequences of divorce (liquidation of property, child custody, alimony, etc.)	Spouses live together: court with jurisdiction of their residence; Spouses live separately AND --there is a child living with one of them: court of child's residence -- absence of children living with them: court of the defendant's residence
C. Rupture of Cohabitation (*rupture de la vie commune*)	Separation for at least 6 years OR insanity (i.e. serious impairment of the mental faculties of one spouse for more than 6 years)	Dispute situation with representative of the spouse who is not mentally capable of making his/her own decisions	J.A.M. for pre-litigation investigation and summary proceedings; Court for divorce decree	Spouses live together: court with jurisdiction of their residence; Spouses live separately AND -- there is a child living with one of them: court of child's residence -- absence of children living with them: court of the defendant's residence

* Juge aux Affaires Matrimoniales

Type of Divorce	1. BASIC CONCEPT	2. TYPE OF PROCEDURE	3. JURISDICTION	4. TERRITORY COMPETENCE-
D. Fault (*faute*)	Proof of incriminating facts; Proof of the *intolerable* nature of such facts	Dispute; Eventually, appointment of a guardian for children (*tuteur*)	J.A.M. for reconciliation, pre-litigation measures, summary procedures; Court for divorce decrees	Spouses live together: Court with jurisdiction of their residence; Spouses live separately AND -- there is a child living with one of them: court of child's residence -- absence of children living with them: court of the defendant's residence

*: *Juge aux Affaires Matrimoniales*

Type of Divorce	5. INITIAL PETITION	6. URGENT MEASURES	7. EXHIBITS SUBMITTED WITH INITIAL PETITION	8 AT INITIAL HEARING
A. Mutual Consent, Joint Petition (*consentement mutuel*)	-Only after at least 6 months of marriage;- not necessary to specify reasons for divorce; - must include mandatory information required by law; - must be dated and signed by spouses and their lawyer(s)	Not necessary; no dispute	Temporary divorce contract and draft of final divorce contract, dated and signed by spouses and their lawyer(s)	Admissibility of the petition: - jurisdiction and territorial competence - verification of spouses' consent (must be true and sincere and freely given) - review of final divorce contract
B. Mutual Consent, deferred in time (*demande acceptée*)	- Presented by the "filing" spouse's lawyer (except for urgent measures); - need not specify reasons for divorce	Upon filing of petition: for spouses: separate residences (eventually with children) for property: conservatory measures such as distainers (*saisies*) with seals (*scellés*) placed on property	Personal report dated/signed by filing spouse (objective statement of facts without qualification of facts nor attribution of responsibilities)	2 possibilities: -No answer, or refusal;delay for answering: 1 month - Acceptance: accepting spouse gives oral confirmation of acceptance of divorce
C. Rupture of Cohabitation (*rupture de la vie commune*)	- Presented by the filing spouse's lawyer (except for urgent measures); reasons for divorce must be objectively specified	Upon filing of petition: for spouses: separate residences (eventually with children) for property: conservatory measures such as distainers (*saisies*) with seals (*scellés*) placed on property	Statement by filing spouse of how he/she intends to meet his/her obligation to help out (*devoir de secours*) abandoned spouse and pay child support	Reconciliation attempt

Type of Divorce	5. INITIAL PETITION	6. URGENT MEASURES	7. EXHIBITS SUBMITTED WITH INITIAL PETITION	8 AT INITIAL HEARING
D. Fault (*faute*)	- Petition filed by the "accusing" spouse's lawyer (except for urgent measures); may or may not give reasons for divorce (*motivation*)	Upon filing of petition: for spouses: separate residences (eventually with children) for property: conservatory measures such as distainers (*saisies*) with seals (*scellés*) placed on property	Documents justifying urgent measures requested	Reconciliation attempt

Chart 1: (cont.) Comparative Chart of the Four Divorce Procedures

Type of Divorce	9. TEMPORARY MEASURES	10. APPEAL	11. SERVICE OF PROCESS	12. PRE-LITIGATION INVESTIGATION
A. Mutual Consent, Joint Petition (*consentement mutuel*)	Those provided for by the temporary divorce contract which are automatically carried out (i.e. specific court order is not necessary)	Within 15 days of the court's decision	Not necessary, no dispute	No pre-litigation proceedings necessary (*mise en état* not necessary); waiting period of a minimum of 3 months and a maximum of 6 months (reflexion period) prior to reiteration of spouses' desire to divorce
B. Mutual Consent, deferred in time (*demande acceptée*)	In case of reconciliation: J.A.M. records reconciliation (*procès verbal de conciliation*). In case of absence of reconciliation: court sets forth temporary measures (separate housing, child custody, alimony/child support) court order recognizes couple's confessions (*double aveu*); the cause for divorce is established; referral is made to the court for consequences of divorce.	Within 15 days of notification of the court's decision	Waiting period (*délai*) begins as of date of court order setting forth temporary measures (3 months for filing spouse, then 3 additional months for accepting spouse), after which time measures set forth become inoperative	J.A.M. is in charge of pre-litigation investigative measures. Any faults shall be considered as shared faults. Members of the families may be heard on child custody. A *notaire* may be appointed to evaluate how much alimony (*prestation compensatoire*) to allocate and also to draft a liquidation scheme

Type of Divorce	9. TEMPORARY MEASURES	10. APPEAL	11. SERVICE OF PROCESS	12. PRE-LITIGATION INVESTI-GATION
C. Rupture of Cohabitation (*rupture de la vie commune*)	In case of reconciliation: J.A.M. records reconciliation (*procès-verbal*) In absence of reconciliation: court sets forth temporary measures (separate housing, child custody, alimony/child support).	Within 15 days of notification of the court's decision	The waiting period (*délai*) begins as of date of court order setting forth temporary measures (3 months for the filing spouse, then 3 additional months for the accepting spouse), after which time measures become inoperative	J.A.M.: all pre-litigation measures; exchange of briefs; new or additional petitions may be made before the court (*demandes reconventionelles*). The J.A.M. may be ordered to investigate. Members of families may be heard on child custody. A *notaire* may be appointed to evaluate how much alimony should be allocated (*prestation compensatoire*) and also to draft a liquidation scheme for property held jointly.

Type of Divorce	9. TEMPORARY MEASURES	10. APPEAL	11. SERVICE OF PROCESS	12. PRE-LITIGATION INVESTI-GATION
D. Fault (*faute*)	In case of reconciliation: J.A.M. records reconciliation (*procès verbal de conciliation*) In absence of reconciliation: court sets forth temporary measures (separate housing, child custody, alimony/child support)	Possible within 15 days of <u>notification</u> of the court's decision	The waiting period (*délai*) begins as of date of court order setting forth temporary measures (3 months for the filing spouse, then 3 additional months for the accepting spouse), after which time measures become inoperative	J.A.M.: all pre-litigation measures; exchange of briefs; new or additional petitions may be made before the court (*demandes reconventionelles*) The J.A.M. may be ordered to investigate. Members of families may be heard on child custody. A *notaire* may be appointed to evaluate how much alimony should be allocated (*prestation compensatoire*) and also to draft a liquidation scheme for property held jointly.

Chart 1: (cont.) Comparative Chart of the Four Divorce Procedures

Type of Divorce	13. EXHIBITS SUBMITTED PRIOR TO COURT DECISION	14. POSSIBLE COURT DECISIONS	15. NOTIFI-CATION OF THE COURT DECISION	16. COURT COSTS
A. Mutual Consent, Joint Petition (*consentement mutuel*)	- Statement certifying the actual performance of the temporary divorce contract - Final divorce contract - Statement concerning the property to be liquidated (*état liquidatif*)	1) Divorce is pronounced. Final divorce contract is judicially approved (*homologation*) 2) Judge dismisses the petition or declares it no longer valid if the petition was filed more than 6 months prior to the decision	Not necessary	Paid as per final divorce contract OR, where stipulated, shared 50/50
B. Mutual Consent, deferred in time (*demande acceptée*)	- Any documents concerning the consequences of the court's decision -Eventually, as a general rule, a contract concerning liquidation and division of property (*liquidation et partage*). Often judges request this but it is not always requested immediately. The tendency is toward a systematic request at some point of the procedure.	Divorce is pronounced on basis of presumably shared faults.	Mandatory. An appeal may be filed within one month of the notification of the court decision. Notification is necessary for this time period of one month to begin.	50/50 except where otherwise stipulated

Chart 1: (cont.) Comparative Chart of the Four Divorce Procedures

Type of Divorce	13. EXHIBITS SUBMITTED PRIOR TO COURT DECISION	14. POSSIBLE COURT DECISIONS	15. NOTIFI-CATION OF THE COURT DECISION	16. COURT COSTS
C. Rupture of Cohabitation (*rupture de la vie commune*)	- Documents and guarantees concerning obligation to aid abandoned spouse (*devoir de secours*) - Medical diagnosis in case of alleged insanity - Eventually, as a general rule, a contract concerning liquidation and division of property (*liquidation et partage*) Often judges request this but it is not always requested immediately. The tendency is toward a systematic request at some point of the procedure.	1) Acceptance of petition: Divorce is pronounced on basis of filing spouse's exclusive fault (the abandoned spouse being "innocent") - Applies where the court has accepted a *demande reconventionnelle* filed by the abandoned spouse 2) Refusal of petition: dismissal of the divorce petition on the grounds that divorce would cause exceptional "hardship" to the abandoned spouse (*clause de dureté*)	Mandatory. An appeal may be filed within one month of notification.	Incurred by the filing spouse

Type of Divorce	13. EXHIBITS SUBMITTED PRIOR TO COURT DECISION	14 POSSIBLE COURT DECISIONS	15. NOTIFI-CATION OF THE COURT DECISION	16. COURT COSTS
D. Fault (*faute*)	- Proof of fault - Documents on the consequences of the court's decision - Possibly a contract on liquidation and division of property (*liquidation et partage*)	4 possibilities: - Court orders an investigation - Divorce is declared as the exclusive fault of one spouse (the "guilty" spouse) - Divorce is declared on basis of "shared fault" - Court dismisses the case When expressly requested by one spouse, the court may keep secret the reasons for divorce (to avoid scandal...) Shared fault may be declared even where no new or additional petition (*demande reconventionnelle*) has been accepted by the court (contrary to divorce for rupture of cohabitation)	Mandatory. An appeal may be filed within one month of notification.	Pursuant to the court's decision. Where there is exclusive fault of one spouse, it is the "guilty" spouse who incurs costs. When it is shared fault, the costs are shared, 50/50.

Chart 2: Effects of Divorce ON PROPERTY AND RIGHTS

Type of divorce	General Effects	Effects of a *demande reconventionnelle**	Duty to aid *(devoir de secours)*	*Prestations compensatoire*
A. Mutual Consent, Joint Petition (*consentement mutuel*)	In accordance with the divorce contract	Does not exist in this form of divorce	None; the divorce contract covers everything	Yes, according to final divorce contract as approved by the J.A.M.**
B. Mutual Consent, deferred in time (*Demande accepté"*)	The general effects are those of divorce for shared fault.	Does not exist under this form of divorce	None; duty to aid is not maintained after divorce	Yes, as decided by the court
C. Rupture of Cohabitation (*rupture de la vie commune*)	The general effects are those for the fault of the filing spouse.	When such *demande* is admitted by the court, the filing spouse shall be deemed entirely responsible for the divorce.	Yes, duty to aid subsists after divorce	Yes, in favor of the "abandoned" spouse. However, the "abandoning" spouse loses all rights to "*prestation compensatoire*". Exceptionally an additional sum (an *indemnité d'équité* may be allowed if married life lasted a significant number of years and one spouse contributed to the other spouse's professional life and success. Intended to indemnify the spouse's work.
D. Fault (faute)	In accordance with the court decision	In accordance with the court order rendered on the merits (*sur la demande principale*)	No	Same as for disruption of cohabitation

*: A counter-attack lodged by a person having been served process.
**: *Juge aux Affaires Matrimoniales*

Chart 2 (cont.): Effects of Divorce ON PROPERTY AND RIGHTS

Type of Divorce	Loss of Marital Advantages	Damages	Loss of rights granted by law OR a contract with third parties
A. Mutual Consent, Joint Petition (*consentement mutuel*)	In accordance with final divorce contract	No possibility of claiming damages. However, the final divorce contract covers *prestations compensatoire*	No
B. Mutual Consent, deferred in time (*demande acceptée*)	In accordance with the spouses' wishes	None	No
C. Rupture of Cohabitation (*rupture de la vie commune*)	The filing spouse automatically loses his/her right, ipso jure. The abandoned spouse conserves his/her rights.	Yes, the abandoned spouse may claim damages if the court has admitted a *demande reconventionnelle*, filed by the abandoned spouse against his/her spouse.	Yes, the spouse having filed for divorce is deemed responsible for the divorce. He/She, therefore, loses all rights granted by law or contracts with third parties.
D. Fault (*faute*)	The "guilty" spouse automatically loses his/her rights if his/her guilt was exclusive. In accordance with spouses' wishes in case of shared fault.	Yes, if one spouse is declared to be exclusively at fault, damages may be claimed against him/her.	Yes, if divorce declared to be exclusive fault of one spouse. No, if shared fault.

Chart 2 (cont.): Effects of Divorce ON PROPERTY AND RIGHTS

Type of Divorce	Sécurité Sociale coverage for non-working woman	Retirement pension paid through Sécurité Sociale to non-working woman	Civil and Military Pensions	Liquidation of the Community
A. Mutual Consent, -Joint Petition (*consentement mutuel*)	As a general rule, divorce engenders loss of rights to *Sécurité Sociale* coverage.	Loss of right to retirement pensions paid through *Sécurité Sociale*	Yes, these shall be maintained.	In accordance with final divorce contract and the *état liquidatif*
B. Mutual Consent, deferred in time (*demande acceptée*)	As a general rule, loss of rights to *Sécurité Sociale* coverage	Loss of right to this retirement pension	Yes, these shall be maintained.	Either as agreed between the spouses in a notarized act (*convention notariée*) or by court order. The J.A.M. may request a *notaire* to draft such a notarized act.
C. Rupture of Cohabitation (*rupture de la vie commune*)	The abandoned spouse maintains his/her rights to *Sécurité Sociale* coverage	Retirement pension rights subsist after divorce	Yes, these are maintained to the benefit of the abandoned spouse	Same as for a *demande accepté* divorce
D. Fault (*faute*)	As a general rule, loss of rights to *Sécurité Sociale* coverage	Loss of right to this retirement pension	Yes, these are maintained in case of shared fault. However, these are maintained only in favor of the "innocent" spouse where the fault is deemed to be the exclusive responsibility of the guilty spouse.	Same as for *demande acceptée* divorce

Chart 3: Effects of Divorce ON THE PERSON OF THE SPOUSES

Type of Divorce	Use of husband's family name by ex-wife	300 day period during which divorced woman may not remarry AND exceptions to this rule (*délai de viduité*)*
A. MUTUAL CONSENT, Joint Petition (*consentement mutuel*)	According to the spouses' agreement	The 300 day period begins on the date of the initial hearing during which the *J.A.M.* approves the couple's temporary divorce contract.
B. MUTUAL CONSENT, deferred in time (*demande acceptée*)	Agreement of the husband or as authorized by the *J.A.M.*	The period begins on the date of the hearing at which time the separate residences of the spouses were established.
C. Rupture of Cohabitation (*rupture de la vie commune*)	Optional for the woman if the husband filed for divorce	The period is waived in this type of divorce.
D. Fault (*faute*)	Either with the husband's agreement or authorized by the judge when the woman intends to use the husband's name for professional reasons or when the children will be conserving father's name	The 300 day period begins as of the date of the court order establishing the impossibility for the spouses to reconcile their differences.

* As a general rule, a divorced woman may not remarry for a period of 300 days following the dissolution of her preceding marriage to avoid confusion on the paternity of future children.

Chart 4: MEASURES CONCERNING CHILDREN, HOUSING and ALIMONY

(These measures apply to ALL forms of divorce.)

Period from initial filing until divorce is pronounced
Once the initial petition has been filed, an enquiry by social workers may be requested. Urgent measures may be ordered by the court such as a separate residence for the spouse who has temporary child custody. As of the initial hearing, the court may review the social worker's enquiry and decide upon arrangements made between the spouses. An investigation may be ordered (in particular in the case of disruption of cohabitation or divorce for fault) during which the children may be heard and social worker's enquiries or counter-enquiries may be conducted. Temporary measures ordered by the court may be eliminated, modified, completed. Often the judge will declare temporary measures as permanent upon divorce, so this period is fundamental. His/her criteria will be the "temporary" success or failure of the temporary measures implemented.
Divorce decree may include the following measures:
The spouse who owns the family residence may be forced to grant a loan to the spouse having child custody. Measures guaranteeing the payment of alimony may be court-ordered or set forth by the divorce contract. A lump sum amount to be paid in capital may be allocated as alimony rather than payment of a monthly amount. Additional support for children (*pension alimentaire*) may be allocated. The amount of alimony (*prestation compensatoire*) to be paid to the spouse having child custody shall be determined in particular by the amount of time spent relating to the children's education.

Section 2: DIVORCE MEDIATION

by Ellen Grandsard
Child and Family Therapist, Family Mediator

Divorce is a process involving profound emotions. It is rarely simple with a clearcut beginning and end. The issues to be negotiated and agreed upon involve intense emotional conflict. Attorneys often do not have the time or training to deal with couple or family dynamics or to handle the intense emotions churned up during a divorce. The divorcing couple usually need emotional support as well as solutions to their differences and an end to the pain of emotional distancing and conflict. Instead, they can find themselves quickly drawn into an intense battle. As one judge/pioneer of family mediation put it, "filing for a divorce often intensifies family conflict." (see Irving, p.11)

Background

Divorce mediation was developed as an alternative to the legal adversarial system. It is a way to reduce the destruction and hurt suffered by families during the difficult transitional period when the family system is undergoing profound change. Introduced and practiced over seventeen years ago in the U.S. and Canada by attorneys, jurists, social workers, marriage and family counselors and therapists, divorce mediation has been officially adopted by the courts in Canada and in certain states of the U.S. (i.e. California) where it has become an integral part of the divorce process. Divorce and family mediation exists in Israel, England, Holland, Belgium, and Germany, and it has been recently introduced in France.

While a lawyer's role is generally to defend <u>his</u> client's interests to the best of his ability, the mediator has the interests of <u>both</u> parties at heart, and seeks to create a situation where neither side loses. Good attorneys, moreover, prefer to avoid involving their clients in destructive conflicts, and therefore welcome the assistance of a neutral, third party who is trained in family dynamics.

What is Mediation?

Divorce and family mediation focuses on decreasing the potential harm to parents and children during the different stages of divorce and post-divorce. Intervention by the mediator is geared toward helping the couple reduce conflict and bitterness connected to separation and divorce so that agreements and decisions can be reached more rationally and congruently.

It also focuses on empowering each member of the couple to shape his/her post-divorce life. Disagreements are brought out openly. Accusations are mitigated so that practical, equitable decisions can be made with both parties actively participating in those decisions. Instead of concentrating on past mistakes and hurts, <u>mediation aims to mobilize the couple's positive resources for better communication.</u> Such mobilization leads to negotiations and compromises which will enable the couple to construct their future lives separately.

Emphasis is also placed on assisting the couple with solving problems, with facing but mitigating their recriminations, and with reducing guilt and desire for revenge so that they can each rebuild their self-esteem more rapidly and move toward a positive post-divorce situation.

What Can Be Expected from a Mediator

A mediator must have training in the field of divorce and family mediation. It is preferable that she/he have experience and skill in dealing with family dynamics, conflict resolution and preferably have a systems approach to family problems.

She/he should be a highly skilled listener, a good communicator, be able to connect with clients, and empathize with the couple or family situation while remaining neutral.

She/he should create an atmosphere where disputing, angry partners can feel safe to bring up painful personal issues. She/he must be able to contain the discussions in a positive and controlled atmosphere and empower people in conflict, helping them to re-establish a fairer balance of power.

The divorce mediator should enable the couple to find positive elements in their past life together, aiding them to move away from a need for retaliation and revenge. She/he should help spouses mitigate blame and guilt in order to develop an equitable balancing of resources to go on with their lives.

A mediator looks for points of agreement but remains neutral and does not make decisions for the couple. She/he must help them to negotiate effectively with each other, be able to suggest topics for discussion, reinforce positive movement toward agreement and shift topics when necessary. She/he must be non-judgmental and a skillful negotiator.

The Children

The children of divorcing parents will probably benefit the most from divorce mediation. They can suffer deep psychological damage from the confllicts of their parents during and after divorce. (see Wallerstein)

Through mediation, damaging custody battles can be avoided and both parents can be helped to keep the child's interests foremost. Parents need to be reminded that children should not be asked to take sides and that children need a close relationship with BOTH parents. They need to feel that their parents will care for and cherish them during and after the divorce. In mediation, parents can be helped to talk to their children and help them understand that both parents love them even though the family can no longer live together and that the child is not responsible for this decision. A child needs to be reassured that neither parent will ever abandon him/her even if they do not live together.

People may be marriage partners for a while but they are **parents forever**. Concerning future living arrangements, children should not be put in the position of having to choose one parent over the other. A sensitive and skilled mediator seeks to ascertain from children their ideas and feelings about future living arrangements and then, such information is incorporated into suggestions to the parents as to what the optimal custody and visitation might be. Throughout the process, the mediator remains neutral and non-judgmental, keeping the focus on the best interests of the child.

Three Models of Mediation: Therapeutic, Structured and Labor-based

There are three basic models of mediation used currently in the U.S.A.: therapeutic, structured and labor-based. The goals are to draw up an equitable divorce settlement as regards the following issues:
Child custody and child support
Division of property and assets
Spousal support and the form it takes
Tax liabilities and payment: Social Security and insurance benefits

In all three models, it is recommended that during the mediation both members of the couple agree to suspend the litigation process. In France, lawyers and judges are sometimes reticent to do this, but if the mediation begins early enough in the divorce process, a compromise can be obtained more easily. The divorcing parties should openly discuss all relevant information pertaining to the custody of their children or to decisions concerning their assets and revenue. The couple often signs an agreement stating that the process of mediation has been explained clearly to them, and that they understand that none of the information brought up during mediation can be subpoenaed as evidence in the legal process.

In the therapeutic model, the couple's adjustment to the divorce is assessed and mediation is delayed until those issues are addressed. The child's interests are realistically interpreted and communicated to the parents. The welfare of the children becomes of paramount importance. This model of mediation is often called "premediation" by mediators who are using a generic model for mediating a settlement. (see Brown)

Structured mediation, was introduced in 1978 by O. Coogler, an attorney with family system and T.A. training. This model focuses on maintaining negotiations between spouses at a balanced and goal-oriented level, and relies on a specific set of rules and procedures to guide the process. Compulsory arbitration is used when the couple arrives at an impasse since the mediator will not proceed to mediate a new issue if the previous one has not been resolved. The couple must sign an agreement to attend ten sessions together, usually spaced once a week for two hours. The negotiations proceed from issue to issue in a set order. (see O. Coogler)

The labor-based model focuses on the process of negotiation itself rather than on the welfare of the children or family. Divorce mediators who use a labor negotiation model are likely to reserve closure on major disputes until agreement on the entire package has been reached so they can trade off items between and within conflictual areas to reach a final agreement. (see Haynes)

The three models overlap on their basic goals. Divorce mediators in the U.S. and France tend to adopt aspects from each of the three models according to their training and values and to the characteristics of the couple and conflict being mediated. Some more recent trends in divorce and family mediation may use a generic model, thereby adapting one or parts of the above models of mediation to the specific needs of the divorcing or disputing post-divorce family.

To people facing divorce or who are in the throes of the destructive battle of divorce litigation over child custody or property distribution, it may seem difficult to imagine sitting down with the opposing party to reach an agreement on such emotionally-charged issues. However, it has been shown over the years that when people are feeling empowered to shape their destinies in a more positive way, they can and will choose to function more responsibly and rationally in the presence of a skilled, neutral third person. The mediator actively intervenes to help the divorcing couple use their creative resources to end useless fighting and free up energy for more productive living.

When to Consult a Mediator

Research has shown that mediation is more successful when decisions are mediated early in the divorce process before escalation has begun. This is usually within the first two weeks after one or both members have filed for a divorce. (see Kaslow)

When a couple has separated, a mediator should be consulted to set forth the grounds for a temporary agreement and thus reduce future misunderstandings and serious conflict. Some of the most bitter litigation battles result from couples living separately without a clear-cut separation agreement.

When one or both members of the couple are seriously considering divorce, they can consult a divorce mediator (as well as a couple or family therapist). Although mediation is not therapy, more and more mediators are trained to practice premediation as the first phase of divorce and family mediation. The mediator needs to evaluate the couple's capacity to enter into mediation as well as their decision to separate or divorce. This phase is considered therapeutic and is practiced by therapist-mediators. A therapist-mediator is often trained in systemic family therapy as well as in divorce and family mediation.

If the couple is in therapy, the therapist can suggest a mediator. Some couple and family therapists who are trained mediators feel at ease to move into the premediation phase with the couple. Others prefer to refer the couple to a mediator elsewhere. In the past, therapy often stopped when the couple decided to separate, but now therapists are realizing the importance of continuing to help both members of a couple as they go through divorce. This is called divorce therapy.

During the premediation phase which is therapeutic, the strengths and weaknesses of the marriage are analyzed as well as the couple's readiness to end the marriage. Communication and negotiation skills are analyzed and enhanced.

Some couples in the midst of the endless court battle should choose mediation if they begin to see a no-win destructive situation emerging. As mentioned earlier, mediation is particularly helpful for ending destructive battles arising over child custody.

Mediated decisions tend to be respected by the couple and accepted by them for a longer time period than mandatory decisions made by the court since both parents have worked to fashion the agreement themselves.

What is the Role of the Attorney in Divorce Mediation?

When divorce is being considered, both parties need to consult an attorney to learn about the procedures of divorce and to understand what they will need to negotiate as well as their legal rights in the divorce settlement.

Ideally, the mediator works with an advisory attorney who can be consulted at any stage of the process to give legal counsel to the divorcing couple. The attorney may be asked to counsel both parties and, she/he will write up the mediated agreement in legal terms. (Note: Only lawyers can produce the legal papers necessary toward divorce. Be wary of anyone else who says she/he can. Only use a reputable and established lawyer whose credentials are known to you.) She/he can also then represent both members of the divorcing couple in court. Each member of the couple may prefer to consult his/her own lawyer or lawyers. BUT, it is essential that the lawyers consulted agree, in spirit and in practice, to foster the mediation process. The lawyer(s) must be able to work with the mediator towards the mutually-agreed-upon goals. She/he must also agree to work with the best interests of the family in mind and be amenable to working within the mediation process when the couple seeks legal advice.

Family mediation (*la médiation familiale*) is relatively new in France. The first European Congress on Divorce and Family Mediation took place in Caen in December 1990. In France, lawyers may be hesitant to recommend a procedure about which they know very little. However, divorce mediation was developed by attorneys, judges and other professionals dealing with family conflict and violence. These professionals, because of their own or their clients' experiences, wanted to shorten the divorce process which often includes long, annoying, discouragingly hopeless and destructive battles between fighting spouses. Studies in other countries have shown that many lawyers feel that a mediation service has prepared clients to better understand the issues, has reduced the clients' emotional turmoil thereby helping them to use legal services more appropriately. (see Irving)

Many attorneys have discovered that the skills of a mediator and of a therapist can enhance their work with divorcing couples. Moreover, some lawyers are also trained as divorce and family mediators. Often a lawyer will refer clients to a mediator when she/he reaches an impasse. Currently, the trend is toward a multi-disciplinarian approach: attorney, mediator, judge and therapist working together to help resolve family conflict.

How to Choose a Mediator

French social workers, family and couple counselors, attorneys and judges are showing more and more interest in developing new ways of dealing with family conflict. Training in family and divorce mediation is available for professionals. Some sectarized public mediation centers have been set up in the Paris area and in the provinces. Some deal uniquely with child-custody disputes, some with helping divorcing families. There are also private mediation centers. (See Useful Addresses and Resources.)

The cost and duration of mediation depends on the particular family involved but is generally less on both counts than for a long, dragged-out court battle, as in a divorce for fault. The process is time-limited to a maximum of one year: ten sessions or less with two hours per session. Since the couple is present during the hours charged, they can calculate their final bill accurately.

When choosing a mediator, ask about their credentials and experience.

Conclusion

Divorce and Family Mediation is not a panacea. Some couples need to fight out their differences before they can get further in the process of ending the marriage. Couples using the procedure of "mutual consent" (similar to the concept of "no-fault" divorce in the U.S.) sometimes skim over the issues too quickly in order to get to an agreement. Although conflict has been avoided, it may be hovering below the surface and is not always addressed nor resolved by this procedure. Often, within a year after the divorce is pronounced, this unresolved conflict surfaces and the couple goes back to court. It is rare for a family to go through divorce without experiencing some conflict over the issues to be settled.

When faced with a divorce, it is recommended to consult a family and couple therapist or a divorce and family mediator. Even if your spouse refuses to accompany you, go yourself. It may help prevent years of unnecessary emotional damage and scarring.

Divorce should not be a tragedy. However, it is one of the most painful of life crises. Mediation is a process whereby family members participate in forming the agreements which will positively influence the family as it enters a new stage of life.

Divorce mediation is consonant with a philosophic orientation that places great value on self-determination and self-actualization in promoting recovery from an often traumatic life event.

Bibliography and suggested reading

- Babu, Anne. *"La Médiation Familiale: Un Nouveau Service pour les Parents en Instance de Séparation ou Divorce"*. *Le Groupe Familiale*, N° 120, Paris 1988.

Bastard, Benoît and Cardia-Voneche, Laura. *Le Divorce Autrement: La Médiation Familiale*. Paris: Editions Syros, 1990.

Brown, S.M. Models of Mediation. Family Therapy Collections, 12 48-64.

Carter, Elizabeth and McGoldrick, Monica. The Family Life Cycle: A Framework for Family Therapy. New York: Gardner Press, 1980.

Coogler, O.J. Structured Mediation in Divorce Settlement. Lexington, Mass.: Lexington Books, D.C. Heath and Co., 1978.

Folberg, Jay and Taylor, A. Mediation: A Comprehensive Guide to Resolving Conflicts without Litigation. San Francisco: Jossey-Bass Publishers, 1984.

Hayley, Jay. Uncommon Therapy: The Psychiatric Techniques of Milton Erickson, M.D. New York: W.W. Norton and Co., 1973.

Haynes, John M. Divorce Mediation: A Practical Guide for Therapists and Counselors. New York: Springer, 1981.

Irving, Howard. Divorce Mediation: A Rational Alternative to the Adversary System. Toronto: Personal Library, 1980.

Kaslow, Florence and Schwartz, Lita: The Dynamics of Divorce. New York: The Free Press, 1988.

Johnston, Janet and Cambell, Linda. Impasses of Divorce. New York: The Free Press, 1988.

Mnuchin, S. Families and Family Therapy. Cambridge: Harvard University Press, 1974.

Neckles, Raleigh W. and Hedgepath, Joanne. "A Generic Model for Divorce." Journal of Divorce and Remarriage, Vol. 17, No 1/2, 157-169.

Satir, Virginia. Conjoint Family Therapy. Palo Alto: Science and Behavior Books, 1964.

Wallerstein, J.S. Surviving the Breakup: How Children and Parents Cope with Divorce: New York, Basic Books, 1980.

_____. Second Chances: Men, Women, and Children a Decade after Divorce. New York, Ticknor and Fields, 1989.

Watzlawick, P., Beavin, J.H., Jackson, D. Patterns of Human Communication, A Study of Interactional Patterns, Pathologies and Paradoxes. New York: W.W. Norton and Co., 1967.

Whitaker, Carl and Napier, Augustus. The Family Crucible. New York: Bantam Books, 1980.

La Médiation Familiale: Actes du 1er Congrès Européen. Caen, France, 1990.

Section 3: PERSONAL COMMENTARIES ON DIVORCE

[Note: All the commentaries were written anonymously except for the introduction by Judy Stewart-Vidal.]

Commentary on Divorce - 1
by Judy Stewart-Vidal

Introductory Comments Recorded Upon Inception of the Project

The purpose of this section of the AAWE Living in France series is to help American women find their way through the maze of legal and administrative questions which may arise as they contemplate getting a divorce in France. We will map out what you can expect and help you get information which may not be readily available or easy to find. We will share our own experiences and try to identify pitfalls due to cultural differences. Finally, we hope this guide will enable you to cope with divorce.

As preparation for childbirth alleviates anxiety and facilitates delivery, so knowledge of divorce proceedings can help you get through a divorce with minimum trauma. Divorce creates stress; living in a foreign environment while going through a divorce only adds to this stress. Knowing what to expect can be a godsend.

When I decided to get a divorce, my natural instinct was to try to find out more about the subject. Since I had no one to talk to, I bought several books for four hundred francs. The books were not ideal. One was tedious to read and no help at all. The second dealt with divorce as it relates to children. By the end of the first two hundred depressing pages, I had become convinced that my kids were going to be scarred for life.

Next, I called up the social worker at the town hall, explained my predicament, and asked what resources were available: addresses, phone numbers, books, articles, etc. After several months, she provided me with half a sheet of paper on which someone had scribbled several names and phone numbers. I immediately called one of them: the "Secretariat Chargé de la Femme". Our conversation went something like this:

THEM: Lady, if you've got a problem, go see a shrink or call the Ministry of Justice. If you're starving to death, you're entitled to free legal aid.

ME: Wait a second. That's not what I mean. Please don't hang up! I was just looking for information on divorce. Books that I could read, or that my kids could read. Or, the address of a local resource center or support group...."

THEM (now much more snotty): Your personal life is none of our business, Madame. Every case is different. It's impossible to generalize....

Great was my frustration. I KNEW I wasn't nuts. Resource centers DID exist in the United States. I distinctly remembered having seen paperbacks on divorce with insights and tips for novices on bookshelves there. Could such information NOT be available in France??

Unfortunately, the answer was yes. I could not find the equivalent of Laurence Pernaud's J'Attends un Enfant on divorce, nor a guide similar to Paris Pas Cher, because divorce has not yet been universally accepted here. One out of four couples separates, and one out of five children comes from a broken family, but the French public has yet to deal with the issue of divorce. Perhaps this delay is due to the fact that France is a Catholic country.

France and the United States look less and less different. The way people dress, eat, talk and live is more and more alike. You think that you know French people and that they know you. People may even comment on how well you have adjusted to France. You may even think of yourself as being totally assimilated. I would like to suggest that this impression is only an illusion. Cultural differences must not be underestimated, especially at such a difficult time in your life. Beware: you remain an American, brought up in a different culture. Your identity, references and values are different. Roots have a funny way of surfacing in moments of crisis. Recognizing beforehand that different reactions are programmed in you can be a first step towards learning to cope.

What are some of these differences? A willingness to talk about one's problems without becoming "the problem". A certain openness that the French tend to find childish and inappropriate. American women like to get together to solve problems. This propensity may be perceived as infantile. To some French people, our practice of discussing problems presents a threat to the status quo.

As far as the subject of adultery goes, the word "*marivaudage*" says it all. What REAL Frenchman hasn't had a few affairs?

Finally, let's consider Puritanism. Americans follow the rules and see no reason not to. The French seem to rejoice in finding new ways of bypassing regulations.

Another cultural difference: the French excel in the art of compromise. To Americans, "*l'art de ménager la chèvre et le chou*" tends to sound more like a dirty deal than an indication of mental prowess.

The word of the law is somewhat sacred to Americans. Maybe that is why lawyers in the United States are so powerful and expensive. Lawyers in France are cheaper, and in my opinion, less inventive and energetic.

All these cultural differences need to be taken into consideration as one approaches divorce proceedings.

A few more observations, gleaned from my experience:

Tell your children the truth. It's amazing how they can take it. Kids tend to feel guilty and need to be talked to, no matter how young.

If you are the one who wants out of the marriage, you will probably be overwhelmed with feelings of guilt. If he's the one who wants out -- and has probably already gone off with someone else -- you will feel rejected, worthless, angry, frustrated, ashamed. If you BOTH want out, beware of "mutual consent". (Editor's note: We were unable to contact the writer for elaboration on this point. We have heard, though, that it is advisable to have TWO lawyers for "mutual consent" divorces, your lawyer and his lawyer.)

Your husband may feel guilty. Feeling guilty can make men behave in pretty strange ways. They can become ugly. Understanding this tendency can help you realize that you are not necessarily the target or the victim. Also, beware of the Frenchman's education: the French are not taught to express feelings or to analyze their emotions. This factor needs to be added into the equation.

Make time to take care of yourself. Get enough sleep. Eat well. Buy yourself a new dress. This advice may sound silly but you are going through a tough time, and such attention DOES make a difference.

Find a support network. Many women have been through divorce. Getting them to share their experience is valuable.

Think positively. You think of yourself as ugly, worthless, unlovable, a failure, a monster. All of these feelings are common. You are not the exception.

Get some therapy.

Learn the jargon before choosing a lawyer. You will feel less foolish and dependent on his or her knowledge. You will also know how to ask the right questions. Don't hesitate to shop around. You are the client. Know that the style these days is *divorce à l'amiable*: the courts are overwhelmed; dragging out divorces is everyone's nightmare.

At difficult times in life, we feel lost and quite alone, even more so when we do not feel fully acquainted with our environment. The experience is scary. Help yourself by getting information. Read. Talk to other people who have been through divorce. Get out. Don't stay alone with your fears and doubts. Don't let yourself remain ignorant.

And, last of all, know that yes, there IS life after divorce!

Commentary on Divorce - 2

Reflections After a Year of Divorce

There's a line in a Chris deBurgh song that goes something like this: "We can't live together and we can't live apart." I guess it summarizes the way I felt about my French husband when I decided to ask for a divorce.

I got married a few days after my graduation from college and moved to Paris. I never felt at home here. Instant ambivalence would describe my attitude, I guess. Things got worse, rather than better. Depression set in.

After ten years, my husband had an affair, which lasted one year. If we had both been living in America, I think I would have left then. But, he was an excellent father. And, I loved him. So I stayed ten more years, not wanting to put an entire ocean between him and the children: the Atlantic Ocean Factor.

Finally, I made up my mind that I wanted to move back to the United States. My anger at the betrayal was eating away at our relationship. The only way out seemed divorce.

He suggested that we keep up appearances -- stay married in name, but go our separate ways. I thought this was an awful idea and didn't want to even consider it. When I insisted on divorce, he got mean.

I suggested the quicker *divorce à l'amiable*, thinking it would spare everyone pain and anguish. That was a mistake. After being a homemaker for twenty years, I found myself confronted with the reality that the man whose house I had kept and whose children I had raised -- the man for whom I had sacrificed my country and a possible career -- planned to give me nothing. Finally, he was shamed into agreeing to a small amount which barely covers the rent. For six years. None of his retirement am I entitled to. [Note: See "Wills and Inheritance", p. 200, *Pension de Réversion* and "Retirement in France", p. 133.]

My ex-husband took the divorce like a slap in the face. As far as he was concerned, I died the day the divorce was pronounced. I was no longer a member of the family

No one seemed to understand what I was going through. Even my own mother kept explaining away his behavior. The children were living through their own private hell and refused to sympathize. The subject of my difficult adjustment to the divorced state became taboo. "You wanted this divorce," they would cry. "Stop complaining."

Despite all the trauma, I believe I did the right thing. Divorce is not the way you think it will be, though. It's MUCH harder. I do not think that anyone who has not lived through it can fully understand.

I miss my ex-husband in funny little ways. I miss his friendship. I miss his smell and his sense of humor. I miss having our family together. At Christmas, for instance. I miss him in bed. I lived with him for half my life. That's a long time.

Basically, my husband and I were coming from different cultural directions. I thought of divorce as something people did when they couldn't live together anymore. He saw divorce as a horrible stigma not to be revealed to anyone. I expected to be able to discuss the children with him. I expected to remain friends or, at least, be on speaking terms. This is not the case.

If you are considering divorce, think it all out carefully first. Make sure you can deal with lots of unexpected punches which life will throw. Try to get your husband to attend counseling with you first. (Mine refused.) Make sure you have a network of friends who will be there to listen. If your husband is "at fault", go for the throat with a good lawyer so that you, too, will be financially secure. Know that it will not be easy.

Two of my children are now at college in the United States. When my ex-husband drives the third back after a weekend visit, he calls the other two on his car phone. They sit out there, in front of my apartment, chatting. I am excluded. I can no longer afford the transatlantic conversations. He knows it. This weekly call is part of the humiliation. Watching this mean side in him develop is the hardest part of all. When I complain, my mother says, "Now, dear, aren't you glad you had the courage to divorce such a man?"

Part of me is. Part of me isn't.

Commentary on Divorce - 3

I've always found that my own divorce (from 1981 to 1986) is mostly inapplicable to others in its nature -- sordid, sadistic, with physical and mental violence, bribery, perjury, etc. My ex-spouse appealed the divorce, then took it to the *Cour de Cassation*. He was condemned in criminal court for violence, then did what one does to "get the sentence relaxed". He had me sentenced to a year in prison since my daughter refused to open the door when he came by to "exercise visiting rights". My sentence was suspended for five years, provided he didn't simply request application of it. There was no hope for my marriage, however I do recommend that anyone considering divorce attempt to salvage a marriage first. Thinking long and hard is not enough. Here is what you must do:

Take two sheets of paper, divided in the middle. On the left side of one, write "Why I Should Try To Salvage". On the right side, write " Why I Can't Salvage". Title the second sheet "Problem-Solving".

Conduct brain-storming sessions with any friends or family who may be of help. The object is to see what problems in the TRY column can begin to get worked on sufficiently to be transferred to PROBLEM-SOLVING. Some problems to consider are the following:

1) Do you still love your husband and/or respect him? If your husband's extramarital affairs are the major reason for seeking a divorce, you should put this issue in the TRY column, no matter how difficult. Enduring affairs may be less painful than all that you will suffer if you do get a divorce. You may reach an agreement: either he stops, or you decide affairs are okay. Some women, who obtained a divorce for infidelity, bitterly regretted their choice to divorce after discovering their new man did the same after a certain time.

2) Consider the consequences on your children of even the best possible divorce: short-term and long-term (a divorce can have consequences on not only their future relations with you but the kind of mate they will choose).

3) Can you bear to see your children spend weekends, holidays and vacations with your ex-spouse?

4) Can you deal with a drastic change in lifestyle? Remember, a wife and children usually get about one-fourth of a husband's DECLARED revenue.

5) If you plan to live with a new man, try to foresee the problems which may arise, especially when your children and his children visit at the same time.

6) Do you have a profession? Have you worked before? Can you find work and support yourself?

7) Consider the social context here in France: French women guard their husbands zealously and try to keep separated or divorced women at a distance - - including former friends.

8) Are you being realistic about the complications involved in being a single parent: raising children while holding down a job and attempting to " start a new life"?

9) If your divorce is contested and things get nasty, are you strong enough emotionally to put up with continual belligerence with low blows? Some women underestimate the effect of such treatment. I have seen friends go from depression to madness to suicide attempts.

10) Imagine what your life will be like after the divorce. Try to judge whether you STILL think it would be better than continuing in your present situation.

Finally, once you have finished filling out the two sheets of paper, get all the help and advice available. Find a support group. Try therapy and counseling. Women have been helped by marriage clinic seminars: some reconcile temporarily or longer; some divorce but they feel satisfied that they had explored every possible way to reconcile.

If, afterwards, you remain absolutely certain that you want to get a divorce and cannot love your husband, and/or have no respect for him, start thinking about your grounds for divorce.

Other Tips and Advice

- KEEP THE DIVORCE PLANS SECRET from mutual friends, even if you and your spouse are filing for divorce by mutual consent.
- Read up on divorce in France.
- Understand the essential differences between French and American law. I found that one of the most vital differences is that there is no testimony by you, your children, or close family. Evidence is written testimony by "third parties" which even lawyers admit is often perjured and subject to bribes or *gratuités*. You can request that your accuser(s) face you in court to justify their accusations but they can refuse to appear merely by justifying excuses not to come.
- Find out what the judicial climate is in your region. For example, if the place of your permanent residence is Versailles, you are subject to laws applied in the Yvelines department. In the 1980s, Versailles was known to be pro-male and anti-American.
- If you need written testimony, remember that people are more willing to support you orally than in writing. Sometimes a female friend may be pressured by her husband into refusing once she has agreed to help.
- Make a list of every person who might be able and willing to back you up and supply necessary detail.
- Find out as much as you can about similar cases.
- Get the best possible lawyer for YOU AND YOUR CASE. If divorce is being pronounced by mutual consent, the lawyer will have split loyalties. Remember that women lawyers, like women judges, can be just as pro-male as males can be machos!
- Think carefully about when, how, and what you tell the children.
- If you tend, by nature, to avoid unpleasantness, you must try to prepare yourself ahead of time to avoid quasi-paralysis every time you receive an official document. Develop a pragmatic approach. Pretend you are handling the case of someone else. Do each little thing step by step, to get through divorce-related chores like mailing out bills.
- Obtain all possible information from your spouse before he knows you intend to divorce. Afterwards, it may be too late. Better to get too much than not enough.
- Hide all information, letters, etc., about yourself, however innocuous.
- Keep a journal as soon as possible. Write your past history since the beginning of the marriage. Hide the journal.
- Get work with regular hours for as much time as you can to avoid giving in to negative feelings.
- Keep your head above water. Know you can succeed if you have to. Others have.

Commentary on Divorce - 4

Is divorce really the best solution for you? Think very carefully about getting a divorce. It is easier to get married than to get a divorce. You and everyone in your family will be affected both morally and materially.

You will go through a very difficult period. Things will happen to you that you never imagined possible. Your husband could turn into the most cruel, cold, and calculating man. Do not ever despair! You will be surprised: the people you least expected will be there to help you go through up and down times.

It is YOUR decision. Your choice. You must not be influenced by any outside person: not your mother, not your best friend, and especially not your lawyer.

Remember the Girl Scout motto "BE PREPARED"? You have made your decision, so you had better be prepared and not waste any time. The following are some helpful hints:

Most important is your financial situation. Have you saved enough money to survive? A divorce is costly. You will be immediately cut off from any monthly allowance you had been receiving from your husband even before the divorce is pronounced.

Do you have your own bank account?

Are you ready to give up more than 50% of your present living standards? Examples: smaller apartment, less vacation, fewer clothes, no more maids, or summer trip to the U.S., etc.

Do you have projects for a new life? A new job? Where are you going to live? Will you stay in France or in the U.S.A.?

If you decide to go back to the States, have you thought about housing, education for the children, a job, social security, etc.?

If you want to get a divorce in the United States, have you checked your state laws? Each state is different.

You signed a French marriage contract. Be sure to read it carefully.

Will you be able to live alone?

Will you be able to live alone with your children?

If you are already working, will you be able to support yourself on that salary? You will now have to pay the rent, gas, electricity, water, dentist, doctor bills, etc.

Who will take care of the children while you are at the office? Children in France have a lot of vacation. Who will pay for their holidays?

Have all your personal papers in order:

Passports: yours and the children's, French and American;
Livret de Famille;
Check books, personal bank account;
Sécurité Sociale;
Driver's license;
Will;
Taxes.

Know your husband's salary and bank accounts.

Know where extra income is coming from: stocks, real estate, etc. Keep all receipts to show your standard of living: rent you pay for the apartment in which you live, summer home you rented, winter sports, airline tickets, etc.

Keep a copy of your maid's *fiche de paie.*

Keep the receipts of anything valuable you buy such as furniture, antiques, and art objects.

Rent a safe deposit box in a bank to keep all your valuables and personal documents.

Shop around for a good lawyer. Tell him/her the details and ask questions.

If you want to hire a detective, best to check with your lawyer first. Detectives are expensive and in the end may not prove necessary.

The above are helpful thoughts to prepare you for getting a divorce. Once you have chosen your lawyer, she/he will tell you what is best for you. The better you are prepared the easier it will be for you to help your lawyer. You will be doing a lot of the work that you think the lawyer should be doing... but you have to help him/her and be behind him/her all the time to get things moving on.

You must prepare yourself step by step, slowly but surely, all by yourself. The best advice is not to talk to everyone about your divorce. That may be difficult, but it's no one's business. Talking too much may turn out to work against you, so be careful!

Divorce is not a game. You are taking serious steps toward a happier future. You will make it and survive and come out a much stronger person. You are not the first person going through a divorce. Many of us made that difficult decision and survived. Be positive! Smile!

Commentary on Divorce 5

I was married to a Frenchman for eighteen years. We had two children who were aged eighteen and eleven when we got a divorce. We had lived for ten years in France, three in the United States and five years elsewhere. That was eighteen years ago. I now live in Paris. I would like to share my impressions with you of what people can expect after a divorce or separation.

There is likely to be immediate psychological fallout. Reactions will be contradictory and unexpected. These may include a sense of relief and an emptiness, often accompanied by a period of mourning, both for what was and for what could have been. There will be moments of high energy, then moments of paralysis. Often this period is characterized by increased physical and mental fragility. After a divorce, people need to take especially good care of themselves. A lack of physical stamina and a feeling of not being able to cope are normal. If you know what to expect, depression may not hit as hard.

Radical changes and risks may be in the works. After a divorce, many people will have to deal with some of the fears from which they were protected during their marriage. Such fears must be confronted with a certain comprehension and compassion. For example, it may not be easy for a woman to join the work force if she has been at home for many years. Know that others have succeeded. Help is available and should be sought out.

People who have been divorced frequently have identity problems. They worry about their own worth and their place in society. Real assessment may be needed. Support and encouragement from others to explore and create a new sense of self will help.

Children often are supportive during the separation and divorce proceedings only to become real problems afterwards. Difficult behavior may be a good sign, as they may be sensing that you are now free to give them more time and energy.

If you do have children and wish to establish a good working relationship with your ex-husband, avoid using the children to carry messages or requests for money.

Older children can be counted on to work things out for themselves if a basic schedule is set up and the parents don't interfere.

With younger children, it is important to draw up a contract on how they will be raised. Such an agreement can be limited to basic values such as what is acceptable to both parents and where compromise is needed. This contract will be more problematic if fighting about child-rearing serves as a cover for other more fundamental problems. It is important to assess positive parenting in each parent and see how a cooperative arrangement can be attained.

If there is a question of danger or possible neglect, careful and objective evaluation of the situation is essential. Professional help can be sought. Concrete steps must be taken to protect the children.

If you have no children, there may be no reason to remain in contact with your ex-husband since such contact may entail a delay in the creation of a new life. You may want to remain in touch if the problems in the marriage were such that a positive relationship is seen as a desirable and satisfactory solution for both parties.

Know that the problems you had during your marriage will remain problems during your divorce. It is helpful to keep this in mind. People often erroneously believe that a divorce will settle everything.

It is imperative to separate fully from your ex-husband in order to be able to move forward and establish a new life with your children.

Have enough basic income so that the children's standard of living does not change. Many women underestimate how much is needed and are reluctant to ask for adequate support.

Commentary on Divorce 6

Wife's nationality: American
Husband's nationality: French
Marriage: lasted 10 years; all of those years were spent in Paris.
Children: 7 years and 4 years at time of separation; 8 and 5 years at time of divorce.
I have been divorced 2 1/2 years.
I am now living in the United States and plan to stay.

The first thing to remember when marrying a foreigner and moving to his country is that you are at a disadvantage from the beginning.

Differences include:

- expectations of a marriage (yes, French men screw around a lot, but if you put up with it, he won't leave you--and this primarily for financial reasons; however, the double standard originated in France, so don't expect to have meaningful relationships outside the marriage yourself),

- child-rearing and family relations (his family and yours). Unless you are of the same religion (and even then) you are always wrong. Why? Because his mother raised her children differently--look how nice her son has turned out! (Testimonial living proof!). Everyone--from the *concierge*, to the *mamans* at the park, to the lady sitting down on the bus, (while you stand with a bag full of groceries, a babe in arms and another crying because her foot has just been stepped on by a drunk)--knows that American children are raised with no manners.

- the job market. Unless your dream job has been to become a secretary or a teacher of English-as-a-second-language, forget it. That is unless you're *pistonnée*. For women who do get jobs, the hours are long, the pay is low and the work is boring. Also, don't forget the children, the housework, and the cooking, because those will remain your jobs, too.

If you're contemplating a divorce-- let's say you want to leave him, but he wants you to stay--and you have signed a *séparation de biens*, you are screwed.

Get a good lawyer. Once you find a good lawyer, watch him/her very closely because most lawyers are interested in billable hours, so don't count on him/her for anything much except making complications in order to generate more billable hours.

Get help, all the help you can get. Babysitters, *femmes de ménage*, delivered groceries.

Don't be a martyr. Do whatever you need to do to get through this time intact. Buy clothes, go to the hairdresser, eat lunch at restaurants--soon enough you will be very poor and unable to indulge.

Talk to friends. They are invaluable. You will find that some of them fall by the wayside, but others, maybe unexpected ones, will pop up, so talk to them as much as possible.

Plan to move back to the States. The children "need" to be close to their father? Maybe, but more important, you need a life, and life in France for a divorced American woman with kids, a crummy job, no money, a tiny apartment, the ex-husband and his 25-year-old girlfriend who come to take your children to fancy hotels twice a month--if he has time--well, who needs it? Not even the kids.

Commentary on Divorce - 7

Life goes on. Yes, but at what cost? I had never lived alone. It had seemed so natural to take care of my husband, to give him top priority and to be a good corporate wife. I regretted not having children. Suddenly I was alone, with no one to care for. I was BEING cared for: friends and family gave support and love and helped me get my sense of humor back... but I knew that sooner or later I would have to come home, close the door and deal with ME, singlehanded. Something told me to watch out for the cliché of the gay divorcee: I was wary of the cocktail hour and wary of men. But I had finally learned that it was okay to talk about personal matters, and my friends got an earful! Our generation was brought up to "keep things to ourselves" and told that "if you can't say something nice, you shouldn't say anything at all".... Remember Mr. and Mrs. Bridge? Yes, it helps to talk once you've learned how.

Perhaps divorce is a kind of mourning. After all, you lose part of your life... maybe even your identity, especially if you have not worked. Since I had lived abroad (Morocco, Iran, Kuwait, Holland and England) during most of my twenty years of married life, I had had no professional life. But thanks to AAWE, at forty-three years of age, I found a job as director of a relocation company, one of the first in Paris..., and that was fun. Meeting people and helping them, helped me. For the first time in my life, my evenings were free. Since the theater had been my youthful passion and I was on the stage when I met my husband, it seemed right to pick up where I had left off. A friend and I founded "The New American Theater". We did three productions a year for quite some time. But that's ancient history. I'm retired now. Although I'm still busy, I have learned the value of solitude and need more time to myself. It's no longer necessary to fill up every minute of the day and night with action-packed activities. The dear friends are still there, and we still have lots to talk about and lots to learn.

There is one unpredictable event I would like to share with you. After I got over hating my husband for what he had done (you know: the OTHER woman), I actually started to like him again. He remarried and I became involved with someone who meant a lot to me, yet my ex-husband and I began to have lunch together about once a month. We were comfortable with each other again, and it was reassuring.... We had, after all, been married for twenty years. Then, one day I noticed that he wasn't looking well at all. He had cancer and, in six months, he was dead. Talk about mourning! My friends couldn't understand how bereft I felt. How could they? In any case, I am so thankful that my ex-husband and I had made our peace. We all know that hate and bitterness take their toll, and I'm sure that I would be a very different person today if forgiveness hadn't somehow appeared to replace all of that.

And so, my friends, whatever happens, just remember: Life does go on.

Commentary on Divorce - 8

My story might be unusual, but I feel it might help someone who is undergoing divorce.

I was living in the U.S. when I realized that my marriage was over. After many years of counseling and maximum efforts, I had the tough decision of whether or not to move back to France. My French husband had already been transferred there when the cold facts hit me that divorce was the only answer.

I could have stayed in the States. It would have meant starting a new life there from scratch. After much soul-searching and with the support of my parents who felt that my place was near the children's father, I took a plane to Paris. Here, my husband gave me a place to stay until I got back on my feet. The unusual side was that the place of residence was adjacent to his. At first, I was horrified at living so close. In the long run, this has turned out to be a blessing. The children are free to see their father whenever they want. In reality, though, we stick to the traditional schedule: every other weekend and dinner once a week *chez lui*.

The children were helped through the trauma just by the fact that I had moved back to Paris. Although Mom and Dad were no longer together, they saw a new sort of friendship that we have now built up. We both stick to the golden rule of not criticizing each other behind each other's back, and the children no longer have to live in an unharmonious atmosphere. The fighting is over. Sure, it is not the way we would have chosen our lives, but it is a good compromise.

P.S. I am grateful for the outstanding meeting AAWE organized a year ago. I chose the lawyer who spoke. She did a beautiful job. I also made friends at the meeting who were undergoing the same crisis as I. We continue to support each other and are all back to living full, happy lives.

Commentary on Divorce - 9

When my first wife and I finally separated, for good, after twelve years together and two trial separations of short duration, it was not pleasant. Although I was happy, even elated to be on my own and beginning to find myself, the unpleasantness was due to the pain and jealousy and to the continuing problem of trying to make decisions with someone with whom I found making decisions impossible and who felt the same way about me.

Why, I asked myself, should I be upset by someone whom I had been trying to escape for years, by a relationship which I had finally managed to get out of after years of knowing it hadn't been the right one in the first place? Now that we were separated and the emotional complications due to living together had been resolved, why couldn't we be "rational" about dividing the material aspects of our life together?

Well, being an educated, sensitive, politically-correct and guilt-ridden "liberated" male, I initially paid for my sins by giving generously of what I had, in the form of child support. I also left most of the stuff we owned to my wife for the home of my children. Then, I realized how angry I felt and how much I was continuing to give of myself, for all the wrong reasons. I got a lawyer but it was too late: I had to pay a lot for a long time.

Several months later, I began a relationship with a woman who eventually became my second wife. Like myself, she was separated, had a child, understood life's ups and downs, was professionally and politically involved in the right causes and was looking to commit herself to a lasting relationship. Even though it seemed a bit rushed, we thought it was just one of those fortuitous situations that we had found each other at the right time. So, we decided to take advantage of this good fortune.

We were together for nine years before the weight of our individual needs became too great for the relationship to bear. This separation was far more difficult than the first, perhaps because we had had more mature expectations and had invested a lot more in it. Like many men in the U.S. in the early 1980s, I had been seriously exploring what it meant to be a "man". I was going through many changes, and by the time the divorce was over, I had left not only a marriage and a job, but the country, as well!

So, what did I learn from all of this? Several things. **First**, it is unrealistic to think that once you are separated, it will be possible, suddenly, to make decisions that the two of you couldn't make when you were together. The same feelings which made it impossible before the separation will still exist. Actually, the fact that you no longer have to protect yourself from those feelings means that you will be more likely to acknowledge them and let them have their way. At the same time, after a separation, it can be more frustrating, even dangerous, to let those feelings gain the upper hand. You assume that you are now free from all those damned encumbrances when, in fact, the opposite is true. Then, when you find that all those old feelings are still there and are still making you react emotionally and irrationally, you begin to think that there really IS something wrong with you! Expect a bit of a mess.

Second, while you may no longer be a couple in the physical and legal sense, you both are still the parents of your children, and still have the responsibilities that go with parenting, as individuals and as a couple. This is a particularly difficult area. According to many of the theories on the psychology and structure of families, the child has a particular "place" in relation to his parents and in relation to the whole family. The position of the child before and after a separation and divorce is complex, to say the least. It is extremely difficult to maintain an "objective" idea of what is best for our children, but we must try. Often, it is helpful to have an outsider's view. A sensitive teacher, school counselor or skilled family counselor can be of great help.

Third, get a good lawyer. I do not mean "be aggressive or vengeful", but the reality is that you are in the process of cutting the ties that bind. In trying to "even the score", and we all feel that we need to, there are three possibilities: 1) make the other person jealous; 2) line up kids, friends, relatives and others on your side, and 3) get the best deal in a settlement.

Lawyers cannot do anything about the first two items. Those are psychological problems, not legal ones. In fact, avoid any lawyer who says that he or she can. It is not in their competence, and will render any kind of clear judgement impossible. However, a good lawyer is probably the only person who can help you get a just settlement, if such a thing exists. While it may be necessary to assume a tough stance in order to get a fair deal, I do not really advise going for the jugular vein.

Fourth, spend some time with yourself before plunging into another marriage. There are many reasons why a couple's relations do not work out, and no one is ever innocent. It is always easy to see the other person's faults and to blame him/her for the problems. It is much more difficult to see how you contributed to the dysfunctioning of the family. Even if the other person does have serious problems, the question of why you chose to be with him/her and what you gained from the relationship still remains. Moving too quickly from one relationship to another is distracting and consumes too much energy to allow one to seriously explore oneself. Often, we bring the same old problems to a new relationship, increasing the likelihood that it, too, will not work out.

Fifth, life is long, and anger and resentment are, or should be, short. Eventually, you will get over the rage, resentment, sadness and sense of a moment lost or wasted. Under the best of circumstances, you may even wind up with a rewarding relationship with the other parent of your children, the person with whom you spent important time together.

With my first wife, it took about five years before we could establish a civil relationship, and another five before we had that turning-point discussion which enabled us, finally, to accept and value each other. I remember it well: both our sons were with us; there was a palpable feeling of having been cleansed of some ancient disease. It became particularly important for us to have reached that point, for she died suddenly a few years later.

As for my second wife, we have just begun to write each other after more than eight years of being apart. If all goes as planned, we shall meet and make peace this coming summer.

I am married again. I thought that I was finished with this marriage business and that I had too many impossible expectations of the institution. But, one day, it simply did not make a difference to me: I knew that nothing could affect the love and sense of peace and security which I felt and still feel and will always feel with the woman I am with. And so, we had an incredible four-day Breton wedding and are living happily ever after.

I know that I never could have reached this point without having gone through those two previous marriages.

Section 4: USEFUL ADDRESSES AND RESOURCES

Edited by Persis Gouirand

Contributions from Ellen Grandsard, Judy Stewart-Vidal, Carolyn White-Lesieur

The list that follows is not exhaustive. AAWE takes no responsibility for the quality of the services provided by the organizations. We welcome comments, suggestions or additions to this list from our readers.

The list is organized as follows:
- Information and/or documentation pertaining to divorce
- Pertaining to family mediation
- Pertaining to family violence
- Shelters for battered women
- Books for children on divorce
- Publications

Information and/or documentation pertaining to divorce

C.N.I.D.F.F. (Centre National d'Information et Documentation des Femmes et des Familles)
Tel: 43.31.12.34 or 43.31.77.00; Fax: 47.07.75.28 or 47.07.13.45.
7, rue du Jura, 75013 Paris.

- Information by telephone: Monday to Friday from 9:00a.m. to 12:30p.m.
- Open: Tuesday through Thursday from 1:30 p.m. to 5:30 p.m.
- Free or minimal-cost information booklets and other documentation.
- Free consultations by appointment Monday and Thursday afternoons.
- Mediation service.

I.D.E.F. (Institut de l'Enfance et de la Famille)
Tel: 40.39.90.03
3, rue Coq-Héron, 75001 Paris
- Excellent library, including books on divorce, children, etc.
- Open Tuesday to Friday from 12:00 p.m. -6:00 p.m.

Fédération Nationale Solidarité Femmes
Tel: 40.02.03.23
102, quai de la Rapée, 75012 Paris

umbrella organization for 50 other organizations, and in particular:
   Violences Conjugales
   Tel: 40.02.02.33
      - a hot line for battered women,, every day from 10 a.m. to 8 p.m.
      - guarantees anonymity

Divorcé(e)s de France
Tel: 45.86.29.61
B.P. 380, 75625 Paris 13 (8, rue Albert-Bayet, 75013 Paris)

- This is a well-established 1901 association that provides legal and administrative information through a monthly bulletin, as well as other services such as lawyer referrals, an information hot line, mail service, and detailed information sheets on a variety of issues. It gives the impression that it is well worth the 350 FF dues.

Association Communautaire en Faveur de l'Enfant du Divorce
Association Sociale du Marais et des Halles
Tel: 42.77.14.48 (No evening calls)
55, rue des Petits Champs, 75001 Paris
Secrétariat: 86, rue des Archives, 75003 Paris
- Counseling for parents and children.
- Psychological and legal information by mail.

L'Ecole des Parents
Tel: 43.48.00.16; Inter-Service Parents: 43.48.28.28.
5, impasse Bon-Secours, 75011 Paris
- Offers a wide variety of services:

- A telephone line called "Inter-service Parents" which gives free legal, psychological, recreational, and scholastic information from 9:30 a.m. - 12:30 p.m. and from 1:30 - 5:00 p.m. every day except Wednesday afternoons and Thursday mornings. **Tel: 43.48.28.28.**

- A consultation service which operates by appointment every afternoon from 1:30 to 6 p.m. For a fee of 500FF, about-to-be or already separated couples may seek counsel on pre-mediation and mediation as well as other matters. Once the appointment is made, the couple will be sent information on the service prior to their meeting.

- A quarterly review, "*Le Groupe Familiale*".

Association Jean-Cotxet
Tel: 45.75.12.75
96, boulevard de Grenelle, 75015 Paris
➔ Address will be changing soon. Call above number or 43.37.45.60

- Offers two types of services:
1) a team of educators, psychologists, social workers, etc. who assist divorcing parents to find solutions to problems of custody and other issues requiring mediation and provide counseling to children of divorcing parents;
2) Neutral meeting place ("*Lieu-rencontre*") and consultation every week day from 9 a.m. to 7 p.m. and Saturdays from 9 a.m. to 12:30 p.m. and 1:30 p.m. to 5 p.m.

S.O.S. Avocats du Barreau de Paris (Monday - Friday, 7:30p.m. - 11:30 p.m.)
Tel: 43.29.33.00. (Patience and persistence are sometimes required when trying to reach them!)

- Free consultation by telephone with a lawyer

Antenne SOS Avocats pour les mineurs (for children)
Tel: 40.51.77.67.
2, rue de Harlay, 75004 Paris

- Free service for children who wish to contact a lawyer.

La Mairie et les Tribunaux de Grande Instance

- Free consultations for legal information. Contact your city hall or Tribunal for more information.

C.D.I.A. (Centre de Documentation et d'Information de l'Assurance)
Tel: 42.47.90.00
2, rue de la Chaussée d'Antin, 75009 Paris

- Open every week day from 9 a.m. - 12 noon and 2 p.m. - 5 p.m.
- Extensive information on insurance for divorcé(e)s provided free of charge.

Alliance Brisée - Madame Roblin
Tel: 43.50.07.03
59, avenue Georges Clémenceau, 92330 Sceaux

- Open consultations Mondays 10:30 - 11:00 a.m.
- This association provides legal information, moral support, and cultural outings to its members. Dues are 150 FF per year and cover a *Bulletin d'Informations* as well as one free consultation with a lawyer. The association also has two *notaires* on whom it can call.

Féderation des Mouvements de la Condition Paternelle des Pères Divorcés Séparés des Enfants (M.C.P.)
National Headquarters: 144, avenue Daumesnil, 75012 Paris Tel: 43.41.45.18
Paris office: 9, rue Jacques Hillairet, 75012 Paris; M° Mongallet; Tel: 44.73.47.50

- Telephone service providing counsel and moral support every Monday from 6 - 11p.m.
- Branches in the provinces.

FAMILY MEDIATION

****

Association pour la Promotion de la Médiation Familiale (A.P.M.F.)
Tel: 40.60.78.11
14, rue des Frères Morane, 75015 Paris

- Open Tuesdays, 10 - 12a.m.
- Upon request, provides a list of recommended family mediation centers in France.
- Its members are *magistrats*, lawyers, psychologists, parents.

Comité National des Services de Médiation Familiale
Tel: (16) 31.73.67.97
Route d'Aulnay, Le Mesnil-de-Louvigny, 14111 Louvigny

- Upon request, provides a list of recommended family mediation centers in France.
- Its members are associations or organizations that offer family mediation.

****

Centre National de la Médiation (C.N.M.)
Tel: 44.09.03.53
127, rue Notre Dame des Champs, 75006 Paris

- Umbrella organization for 30 mediation organizations and training centers for many kinds of mediation (disputes between neighbors, disputes concerning inheritances, disputes within companies, institutions etc.) including family mediation. (See La Maison de Médiation)

****

Below are a few organizations offering family mediation services. For a more complete list of family mediation services, please contact both the A.P.M.F. and the Comité National des Services de Médiation Familiale for their recommendations.

Association Française des Centres de Consultation Conjugale (A.F.C.C.C.)
Paris branch: Tel: 45.66.50.00; 228, rue de Vaugirard, 75015 Paris
Avrainville branch: Tel: 60.77.67.82; 4, rue de l'Eglise, 91630 Avrainville
- Family mediation services

Association Pères Mères Enfants (A.P.M.E.)
Tel: 30.21.75.55
36, rue des Etats-Généraux, 78000 Versailles
Family mediation service
Subsidized service: low fees

C.N.I.D.F.F.
Tel: 43.31.12.34 or 43.31.77.00; Fax: 47.07.75.28 or 47.07.13.45.
7, rue du Jura, 75013 Paris.
- Family mediation service.
D.A.S.E.S., Service de la Médiation Familiale
(Dir. de l'Action Sociale de l'Enfance et de la Santé)
Tel: 43.07.38.59
15, rue de Chaligny, 75012 Paris
- Free for residents of the 12th Arr.
- Fee for other residents of Paris
Ecole des Parents:
Tel: 43.48.00.16/ Interservice Parents: Tel: 43.48.28.28
5, impasse Bon Secours, 75011 Paris
- Family mediation service and training center.
Institut Européen de Médiation Familiale
Tel: 44.07.22.58
71, rue Saint Jacques, 75005 Paris
- Family mediation service and training center.
La Maison de la Médiation
Tel: 43.26.95.12
38 bis, rue Henri Barbusse, 75005 Paris
- Family mediation service
Resource and Therapy Center
Tel: 42.74.05.67
6, rue Elzévir, 75003 Paris
- Family mediator

The following are centers for residents of these areas:

A.D.E.F. - Médiation 93 Enfance Famille
Association d'Aide à l'Enfance et à la Famille
Tel: 48.44.71.63
19, rue Etienne Marcel, 93500 Pantin

Association pour l'Enfant et le Couple (A.P.E.C. 94)
Tel: 42.07.49.74, Mme Robinet
Tribunal de Grande Instance
rue Pasteur Valéry Radot, 94011 Créteil Cedex

Centre de Médiation Familiale
Tel: 30.32.94.95
2 ter, place du Marché, 95300 Pontoise

Centre de Soins en Milieu Familiale
Tel: 60.16.57.60
67, route de Longport, 91700 Sainte Geneviève des Bois

HELP IN CASE OF FAMILY VIOLENCE

Organizations

Association pour la Prévention de la Violence en Privé
Tel: 40.24.05.05
6, impasse des Orteaux, 75020 Paris

- Hours: weekdays from 10 a.m. - 8:30 p.m. Consultations by appointment.
- Seeks to treat the perpetrator rather than the victim(s) of family violence.

Association Halte: Aide aux Femmes Battues
Tel: 43.48.20.40.
14, rue Mendelsohn, 75020 Paris

- Weekdays from 10 a.m. - 7 p.m.
- English-speaking counselor on Tuesdays, Wednesdays and Thursdays.
- Welcome center and shelter for battered women.

Fédération Nationale Solidarité Femmes: Violence Conjugale Femmes Info Service
Tel: 40.02.02.23
102, quai de la Rapée, 75012 Paris;

- Weekdays from 10 a.m. to 8 p.m. These hours may be increased in the near future.

Hot Lines

CALL THE THREE ASSOCIATIONS LISTED ON PRECEDING PAGE

AND:

Numéro Vert pour Enfance Maltraité: Tel: 05.05.41.41.
- Takes toll-free (no coin needed) calls **24 hours a day**. Excellent referral service.

Violences Conjugales: Tel: 40.02.02.33.
- A hot line for battered women; every day from 10 a.m. to 8 p.m.

S.O.S. Urgence Maman: Tel: 45.22.38.71.
- 8 a.m. to 8 p.m. Emergency babysitting service.

Inter-service Parents: Tel: 43.48.28.28.
- See *L'Ecole des Parents* in list of Associations above.

S.O.S. Familles en Péril: Tel: 42.46.66.77.
- 8:30 a.m. - 6:30 p.m.
- Crisis line providing psychological counseling for those experiencing marital and family conflicts. More in-depth psychological counseling by appointment. No psychotherapy, but can recommend psychotherapists. English-speaking counselors available.

SHELTERS for BATTERED WOMEN
in Paris and suburbs

(For shelters in the rest of France, call Violençe Conjugales, Tel: 40.02.02.33)

Foyer Louise Labbé
Tel: 43.48.20.40
   - a shelter for women and children in distress located in the 20th arrondissement.

Foyer Flora Tristan
Tel: 47.36.96.48
142, avenue de Verdun, 92320 Chatillon-sous-Bagneux

Foyer d'Evry
Tel: 60.78.45.66
5, square Gutenberg, 91000 Evry

La Maison des Femmes
Tel: 30.73.51.52
31, rue du Chemin de Fer, 95000 Cergy St. Christophe

Meaux SOS Femmes Informations
Tel: 60.09.27.99
100, rue du faubourg St. Nicolas, 77100 Meaux

Le Relais
Tel: 60.60.89.70
5-6, passage des Boutiquiers, 77550 Moissy-Cramayel

Books for Children on Divorce

The source for the following books for children is the <u>New York Times Parent's Guide to the Best Books for Children,</u> by Eden Ross Lipton, Times Books/Random House, 1991 edition.

Brown, Marc and Laurene Krasny. <u>Dinosaurs Divorce: A Guide for Changing Families,</u> Joy Street/Little, Brown: 1986   (Story book)
Cleary, Beverly. <u>Dear Mr. Henshaw</u>, Dell Yearling, 1983.   (Middle reading book)
Dragonwagon, Crescent. <u>Always, Always,</u> New York: Macmillan, 1984.   (Story book)
Fox, Paula. <u>The Moonlight Man</u>, Dell, 1986.   (Young Adult book)
Jukes, Mavis. <u>Like Jake and Me</u>, Knopf, 1984.   (Story book)
Jukes, Mavis. <u>No One is Going to Nashville</u>, Knopf, 1983.   (Early reading book)
Krementz, Jill. <u>How It Feels When Parents Divorce</u>, Knopf, 1984.   (Middle reading book)

* * *

Publications

"Couples pour Bien Vivre Vos Droits", Special issue (N° 60, Février 1993) published by *"50 Millions de Consommateurs"*
and
- *"Divorce"*, Special issue (N° 43, Oct/Déc 1989) published by *"50 Millions de Consommateurs"*.

- Both are highly recommended.

-*"Couple et Famille"*: newsletter published by the Féderation National du Couple et de la Famille, 28, place St. Georges, 75009 Paris; Tel   42 85 25 98.

This organization has published a special issue, *Peut-On 'Bien' Divorcer: Le Divorce par Consentement Mutuel*, as a supplement to issue N° 76, Jan-Fév-Mars 1989.

- *L'Ecole des Parents*: monthly newsletter edited by the association of the same name.

- *Le Groupe Familial:* quarterly review edited by *l'Ecole des Parents* (see list of associations).

- Sheets of practical information published by the *Ministère de la Justice.*

- Recommended.

RETIREMENT IN FRANCE

Section One by Phyllis Michaux and Marilyn Gillet

Section Two by Benoit Besson

ABOUT THE AUTHORS

Benoit Besson is a consultant at William M. Mercer-Faugère et Jutheau, France's leading insurance brokerage company. He advises corporate clients on employee benefits and retirement, as well as individuals on estate planning.

A graduate of the European Business School (EBS, Paris), Benoit has worked in the insurance field in Germany and the United States.

He lives in Paris with his wife, Susan, an AAWE member, and their daughter.

Marilyn Gillet, an AAWE member, hails from Texas where she received her B.A. and M.A. degrees from Rice University. A Fulbright scholarship brought her to France. Later, she received a French government *bourse* to finish her doctorate at the Sorbonne. She was head of several Junior Year Abroad programs including that of the C.U.P.A., Sweet Briar College and Hamilton College. She reviews books regularly for the Houston Chronicle and has written articles and reviews for the "French-American Review."

Phyllis Michaux, born and raised in Washington, D.C., came to France in 1947 to marry her French husband. Judging American citizenship laws as they pertained to her children unjust and impossible to comply with, she joined with other American women in 1961 and founded the Association of American Wives of Europeans (AAWE). Still mindful of this issue and other matters of concern to overseas residents, she is active with the Association of Americans Resident Overseas (AARO) and the World Federation of Americans Abroad (WFAA).

TABLE OF CONTENTS

(continued on next page)

RETIREMENT:
SECTION ONE

By Phyllis Michaux and Marilyn Gillet

The information in this section applies to persons eligible for U.S. Social Security retirement benefits who are planning to reside in France after retirement and, in particular, to women. Section III, "The French Side," applies to persons eligible for French retirement benefits from both private and public sources. It deals basically with the case of salaried employees and their spouses, divorced or widowed. If you are -or were- a member of a *profession libérale,* a store owner, a civil servant, etc., you can get more specific information from the agency to which you paid French *Sécurité Sociale* contributions. A list of can be found on the *ANPE Services Spéciales* page of the Paris phone book.

I.   THE AMERICAN SIDE

People who have worked -or are still working- in the United States and have accumulated U.S. Social Security retirement credits there should write or call the Federal Benefits Unit at the U.S. Consulate, 2, rue St. Florentin, 75008 Paris (tel: 42.96.12.02) and ask that a copy of Form SSA 7004 be sent to them. This request for an earnings and benefits estimate statement should then be sent to:

> Social Security Administration
> P.O. Box 1756
> Baltimore, Md. 21203
> Telephone: USA: 1-800-234-5772

Within six to eight weeks you will receive a complete statement of your earnings and U.S. Social Security contributions to date. Check the replies for accuracy and keep them as records. It is very important to keep accurate records of pay and dates of work, i.e. month and year of beginning and ending a job. To obtain full benefits, you must have worked a minimum of 40 quarters (ordinarily the equivalent of ten years) during which you paid into U.S. Social Security.

You can apply for early retirement from the age of sixty-two. However, if you wait until the normal retirement age of sixty-five or over, the benefits you receive will be higher. The amount of benefits is based on your earnings over a period of years, and the payments are presently adjusted each year as the cost of living rises. You will receive an estimate of your retirement benefits after you send in Form 7004. In some cases, monthly benefits may also be paid to spouses and children of retirees and, in some cases, to divorced spouses.

It is wise to apply for benefits four months before you wish them to start. AT LEAST this much time should be allowed for the handling of your file. However, do not apply in the United States if you plan to reside in France. Apply through the Federal Benefits Office at the American Embassy. To apply, you will need your U.S. Social Security card or a record of its number, your birth certificate, and evidence of recent earnings which have not yet been posted to your SSA Account. The Federal Benefits office will inform you if other papers are needed in your particular case. Under certain conditions, it is possible to go on working after retirement without loss of benefits.

II. TOTALIZATION AGREEMENT

An agreement between France and the United States concerning Social Security taxes and retirement benefits, effective July 1, 1988, may affect people who have worked in both countries. Employees who are still active will no longer have to contribute to both systems. A certificate of coverage issued by one country serves as proof of exemption from Social Security taxes on the same earnings in the other country. People applying for retirement benefits may be able to add credits obtained in one country to those obtained in the other.

If you meet all the basic requirements for full benefits under the system of one country, you will receive regular benefits from that country and will not be eligible for totalization based on combined credits. If you do not have enough credits under the system of one country, you may become eligible based on combined credits. Essentially this relates to making the ten-year minimum requirement for U.S. Social Security retirement benefits or the 150-quarter (*trimestre*) requirement before the age of sixty-five for French *Sécurité Sociale* benefits.

To be eligible to have your U.S. and French work credits combined, you first need a minimum amount of credits. In the U.S., a minimum of 6 quarters (one-and-a-half-years), in France a minimum of one year. If the minimum coverage requirement is met, work credits from the other country may be added. For example, if you apply for benefits from France and have at least one year of French coverage but not enough work credits to qualify for a regular benefit, U.S. coverage can be counted. Depending on your situation, you may receive benefits from both countries or from only one.

However, as an American lawyer in Paris recently pointed out, the real advantage of the Totalization Agreement may be limited to individuals with less than ten years of U.S. Social Security coverage who would otherwise obtain no benefits from the United States.

Windfall Elimination: If you are receiving money from a pension for work not covered by U.S. Social Security, your Social Security benefits may be affected (reduced) by a modified benefit formula. This Windfall Elimination law was created to prevent "double dipping". It will not affect the pension from the job not covered by U.S. Social Security. Contact the Federal Benefits Office if you have any questions on Windfall Elimination or consult a knowledgeable American lawyer.

A copy of the Totalization Agreement between France and the U.S. may be obtained from the Social Security office in the American Embassy.

Enquiries about filing a claim under the provisions of this agreement should be addressed to:

Social Security Administration
O I O-Totalization
P.O. Box 17049
Baltimore, MD 21235

You can also contact the Federal Benefits Office at the American Embassy.

More detailed information on the Totalization Agreement may be obtained from:
Social Security Administration
Office of International Policy
Room 1104, West High Rise
6401 Security Blvd.
Baltimore, MD 21235

The French provisions and benefits will also be explained and processed when you apply for benefits from the French *Sécurité Sociale* system, the CNAVTS (*Caisse Nationale d'Assurance Vieillesse des Travailleurs Salariés*; see section IV. Useful Addresses.)

→ A Note on Medicare:

If you have accumulated enough credits, at age sixty-five, you will be eligible for Medicare. Even though the benefits are not payable outside of the United States, some Americans resident abroad enroll in the program when applying for U.S. Social Security benefits. This gives them coverage when traveling in the United States. In case of a serious accident or sudden illness, a Medicare card facilitates immediate entry into a hospital. Part A (hospital insurance) is free of charge. The premium for Part B (medical insurance) was USD31.40 per month in 1992. Payment of the premium is automatically deducted from the U.S. Social Security benefit check. Except for the initial application at the time of applying for U.S. Social Security benefits, enrollment in Medicare can only be made once a year.

A person who is covered by the French *Sécurité Sociale* system can be reimbursed for health care in the United States (or elsewhere outside of France) provided that original bills or receipts are furnished. The amount of reimbursement, though, is likely to be much lower than the actual American health care costs.

III. THE FRENCH SIDE

A. RETIREMENT

1.Official French *Sécurité Sociale* Retirement Pension (*Assurance Vieillesse*)

a. Eligibility: In order to receive any Social Security benefits in France, you must be at least sixty years old and have been credited for at least one quarter (*trimestre*) during which time you paid into *Sécurité Sociale*. To receive full benefits, you must have paid for 37 1/2 years (150 *trimestres*), or be the mother of three children and have worked for 30 years.

For each child that you raised for at least nine years before he was sixteen years old, you can be credited for two years of employment if you were not working during that time. Maternity leave and, in some cases, paternity leave from work are also counted toward retirement. If you have collected unemployment compensation from the ASSEDIC, your retirement payments continued during this period.

The amount of the benefits is based on the ten highest paid years of one's career and will never be more than 50% of the ceiling (*plafond*) set by the *Sécurité Sociale* (nor less than 25%). For example, in January 1993, the salary ceiling sct by the *Sécurité Sociale* was 12,360FF per month or 148,320FF per year. Therefore, the maximum amount of benefits cannot exceed 50% of this 12,360FF per month. The amount of benefits are increased by 10% for persons who have raised at least three children. Despite this low maximum amount of 6,180FF per month, the *Assurance Vieillesse* of the *Sécurité Sociale* gives the recipient the benefits of sickness insurance coverage (*Assurance Maladie*) for a very low rate of contribution.

If you are at least sixty years old and have a minimum of 150 quarters, you may, under certain conditions, continue to exercise a professional activity after retiring without loss of retirement benefits.

b. Application: Like U.S. Social Security benefits, French retirement benefits are not paid automatically. Application forms can be obtained from your local *mairie* or from the agency (*caisse*) that handles your retirement. Start early. It is well to apply four or more months ahead of your intended retirement date to allow for the processing of your file, but your intended retirement date must be specified on your application.

The first step is to open your file with the *Caisse Nationale d'Assurance Vieillesse des Travailleurs Salariés (CNAVTS)* who will determine your eligibility for a French government pension. This must be done before beginning any formalities to receive benefits from any other *Caisse de Retraite* as these private retirement associations (*caisses*) will need a copy of the CNAVTS application. Although it may take three to four months to receive benefits, payment will be made retroactively to the date of application. So if you expect to be financially dependent upon the revenues, apply early.

It is also <u>very important to keep all your payslips</u>, with the exact amounts and dates. You may request an employment record (*relevé de carrière*) from the *Caisse Régionale d'Assurance Maladie, branche vieillesse,* to make sure their accounts agree with yours. If you live in the Ile de France region, send your application to the *Caisse Nationale d'Assurance Vieillesse des Travailleurs Salariés (CNAVTS).*

2. Supplementary retirement policies: To the regular *Sécurité Sociale* pension is added one or more supplementary retirement pensions (*retraites complementaires*), depending on your career.

If you were an employee, you may be entitled to supplementary pensions paid by one of the agencies (*caisses*) belonging to l'ARRCO (*Association des Régimes de Retraites complémentaires*).

If you were a <u>*cadre*</u>, you might receive one or more supplementary payments if you paid in on the part of your salary not liable to *Sécurité Sociale* tax. These payments would also be handled by ARRCO. To these might be added other benefits from the AGIRC (*Association Générale des Institutions de Retraite des Cadres*). See Section 2 of Retirement by Benoit Besson.

If you have been paying into a complementary retirement fund and want further information, contact the *Centre d'Information et de Co-ordination de l'Action Sociale (CICAS)* of the French department in which you live.

B. *SECURITE SOCIALE* BENEFITS FOR NON-WORKERS

Some persons in low income brackets who are caring for young children or for handicapped adults can qualify for retirement benefits even though they are not employed.

If you have a child under the age of twenty and you do not belong to an obligatory insurance program, you may join a voluntary program by making quarterly payments. Apply at your local *Caisse Primaire d'Assurance Maladie* or *Assurance Maladie Volontaire*.

Women who have raised at least five children but have held little or no employment outside the home may be eligible for the allowance for mothers (*allocation aux mères de famille*). Enquiries should be addressed to the *Caisse Régionale d'Assurance Maladie, branche vieillesse*. This information can be obtained from your local *Mairie*.

If you are over sixty-five (in some cases sixty) and your income bracket is very low, you may be eligible for a minimum old-age pension. This consists of two parts: a basic allowance paid by the *Caisse des Dépots et Consignations* and a supplementary allowance from the *Fonds National de Solidarité*. The latter is not automatic and must be applied for on a special form available at the *Mairie*. This pension is usually only awarded to persons of French nationality.

C. SURVIVORS' BENEFITS (*Retraite de réversion*)

1. *Sécurité Sociale* Pension

Families of a deceased person covered by *Sécurité Sociale* usually receive a fixed sum of money (*capital décès*) upon his/her death.

A widow (or widower) may also be eligible for a part of her (his) spouse's retirement benefits under the *Sécurité Sociale* system. To qualify for this *pension de réversion* of the *Sécurité Sociale*, the recipient must be at least fifty-five years old and the marriage must have lasted for at least two years (less, if there was a child). *Concubin(e)s* are not eligible, but divorcees are, unless they have remarried. If the deceased was married several times, the pension is divided on a pro rata basis according to the duration of each marriage.

Another condition is that the recipient's income must not exceed a maximum limit, revised every year. However, if your application is rejected because your income is too high, you can apply again if it becomes reduced -for instance, because of your own retirement. The amount of the pension is established by a sliding scale and is normally equivalent to about 52% of the deceased's retirement benefits. It is increased by 10% if the recipient has raised at least three children.

Application must be made for the *pension de réversion* on a special form that may be obtained at your local *mairie* or *Caisse d'Assurance Vieillesse*. This form should be sent to the agency that paid the deceased person's retirement benefits. It takes two to three months for payment of this pension to go into effect once the application has been accepted.

2. Retraites Complémentaires: Pension de Réversion

In addition to the *Sécurité Sociale* system, the agencies (*caisses de retraite complémentaire*) that handle supplementary retirement benefits also pay *pensions de réversion.* The conditions of eligibility as well as the amount payable vary from one retirement plan to another. Detailed information may be obtained from the organization from which the deceased received his benefits.

Pension de réversion is normally 60% of the official pension of the deceased. Some agencies (*caisses de retraite)* request the retiree to decide before receiving his pension if he wants the *réversion* or not. It is rare that a person turns it down, but one should be aware that the question may be asked. If the retiree does not choose *réversion*, his pension may be higher.

IV. USEFUL ADDRESSES

AGIRC: Association Générale des Institutions de Retraites des Cadres
    4, rue Leroux, 75016 Paris
    Tel: 45.01.53.20.

ANPE: Agence Nationale pour l'Emploi
    Numerous addresses: see phone book which also gives a
    list of specialized agencies.

ARRCO: Association des Régimes de Retraites Complémentaires
    44, bd. de la Bastille, 75012 Paris
    Tel: 43.46.13.20.

ASSEDIC: Association pour l'Emploi dans l'Industrie et le Commerce
    4, rue Traversière, 75012 Paris
    Tel: 43.45.10.10.
    See phone book for other addresses.

ASSURANCE VIEILLESSE VOLONTAIRES
    c/o CNAVTS (see below)

CAISSE DES FRANCAIS DE L'ETRANGER
    B.P. 100, Rubelles
    77951 Maincy Cedex

CICAS: Centre d'Information et de Co-ordination de l'Action
    Sociale (des Régimes de Retraite groupés par l'ARRCO)
    12, rue Exelmans, 78000 Versailles
    Tel: 39.50.78.38.

CNAVTS: Caisse Nationale d'Assurance Vieillesse des Travailleurs
    Salariés (Région Ile de France)
    110, rue de Flandre, 75957 Paris Cedex 19
    Tel: 40.37.37.37.

CNIDFF: Centre National d'Information et de Documentation des Femmes et des
    Familles
    7, rue du Jura, 75013 Paris
    Tel: 43.31.12.39.

RETIREMENT
SECTION TWO

by Benoit Besson

COMPLEMENTARY RETIREMENT POLICIES

The importance in France of the *répartition*, a non-compulsory pay-as-you-go complementary retirement system, cannot be overlooked. Indeed, as illustrated by the figures below, the higher the salary, the less the retirement benefits funded by French *Sécurité Sociale* conform to the actual amount earned and the more they are funded by the AGIRC and ARRCO complementary retirement organizations (explained in the next section).

We should not neglect the importance of French *Sécurité Sociale* retirement benefits since *Assurance Vieillesse* gives easy and cheap access to medical coverage when one retires. This is no problem for the working spouse since she/he are, by law, incorporated in the *Sécurité Sociale* system, but it could be a real problem for the non-working spouse. It is really important that any spouse work for awhile in France in order to obtain a French *Sécurité Sociale* number and even a small benefit since it will enable the person, for a small fee, to be incorporated into the sickness insurance system. For example, she might become a widow and not have access to her deceased partner's *Sécurité Sociale* retirement benefits if her personal revenue is higher than the salary ceiling set by the *Sécurité Sociale*, but she would like to be incorporated into the French sickness insurance system.

This system, which complements retirement benefits accrued by French *Sécurité Sociale*, will be the subject of the next section.

Chart 1: The decreasing share of *Sécurité Sociale* benefits in the retirement benefits of a *cadre*:

Annual Final earnings	Estimated Pension	Percentage of *Sécurité Sociale* benefits in pension annuity	Percentage of ARRCO-AGIRC benefits in pension annuity
288,240FF	139,943FF	42%	58%
576,480	270,613	24%	76%
864,720	369,578	18%	82%
1,152,960	456,013	14%	86%

(Figures as of 1992. Source: William M. Mercer-Faugère et Jutheau)

V. FRENCH SUPPLEMENTARY RETIREMENT POLICIES BY *REPARTITION*: PAY-AS-YOU-GO PENSION PLANS (*La Retraite Complémentaire par Répartition*)

With the establishment of the French *Sécurité Sociale* system in 1945 and the mandatory participation of all employees, welfare schemes, which previously existed on a private basis, became complementary arrangements designed to provide members with benefits to supplement those provided under *Sécurité Sociale*.

Based on national agreements (*Convention Collectives Nationales*) between employers and unions on employee benefits in 1947, 1961 and 1973, supplementary arrangements are now compulsory for all types of businesses.

Benefits are funded through multi-employer or industry-wide institutions, or sometimes, in the case of very large concerns, on a single company basis.

These supplementary arrangements resemble *Sécurité Sociale* in some respects. For instance, both employers and employees contribute, participation is mandatory, and they are financed on a pay-as-you-go (*répartition*) basis. The arrangements also have some of the characteristics of private plans, notably they are privately administered and allow participating employers certain options concerning the level of contributions and benefits.

The Collective Agreement of 1947 governing the supplementary arrangements makes a distinction between two broad categories of employees:
<u>Cadres:</u> Executive employees with technical or academic qualifications and persons with supervisory or executive duties.
<u>Non-Cadres:</u> Basically, blue-collar workers, clerical employees, and *agents de maîtrise.*
The classification of employees is determined according to a numerical job coefficient. An additional category, *cadres assimilés*, exists for more junior supervisors who are often treated in the same way as *cadre* employees.
Finally, a senior executive category, *cadres supérieurs,* is treated no differently, in terms of legally required contributions, than *cadre* employees.

A. THE AGIRC AND ARRCO INSTITUTIONS

A number of funding institutions (*caisses de retraite*) exist in France. Most are grouped under central organisations as follows:
- For *non-cadre* employees: ARRCO (*Association des Régimes de Retraite Complémentaire*)
- For *cadre* employees: AGIRC (*Association Générale des Institutions de Retraite des Cadres*)
- For *cadres supérieurs* (top executives): RESURCA, IRICASE, Class C AGIRC, IRCAFEX
- For Civil Servants: IRCANTEC

The two principal organisations, AGIRC and ARRCO, act as co-ordinating offices for the affiliated institutions and insure the solvency of these member institutions. Although basically different, they have some features in common:

* There is a minimum mandatory contribution rate. A higher rate, up to a fixed maximum, may be paid by agreement between the employer and the employee. (Contribution rates, once established, cannot be reduced.)

* The AGIRC and ARRCO systems operate on the pay-as-you-go (*répartition*) basis, meaning the immediate distribution of contributions. No capital reserves are accumulated, but these organizations insure their solvency by financial stabilizing devices.

While working, one accumulates pension points. On the day of retirement, the amount of points accumulated will be multiplied by the "point value" (*valeur du point de retraite*) determined by the ARRCO/AGIRC institutions. This "point value" is dependent upon the number of active members contributing to the system versus the number of persons receiving retirement benefits under the plan. This explains why there is concern that with the low natality rate, there will be fewer active people than retirees in the beginning of the 21st century. At the time of the adoption of the collective bargaining/national agreements (*Conventions Collectives Nationales*) in 1947, the *répartition* system was selected because there were many more active people than retirees.

After retirement has begun, and to keep up with inflation, the "point value" is re-evaluated, and a new value is assigned by ARRCO/AGIRC each year.

Other common features of the ARRCO and AGIRC organizations include:

*Free pension points may be granted for service prior to a company's joining an institution or *caisse de retraite* and also for periods of unemployment with compensation by ASSEDIC unemployment benefits.

*Normal retirement age is between sixty and sixty-five, providing the number of "working or validated" years corresponds to *Sécurité Sociale* requirements. There is a provision for early retirement but with a reduced pension.

*Widow and orphan's *réversion* pensions are payable proportionately to the deceased employee's accrued pension points at the time of his or her death, either before or after retirement.

*The institutions are managed by a Board of Directors composed of elected representatives of the members (employers and employees).

In addition to these common features, the ARRCO and AGIRC associations have some distinguishing characteristics, examined in the next two sections.

1. AGIRC-- *Association Générale des Institutions de Retraite des Cadres*

The AGIRC groups a number of institutions that must all follow the same rules established by this association.

a. Contributions

Under the AGIRC plan, the minimum mandatory contributions are due on earnings in excess of the *Sécurité Sociale* ceiling and up to the AGIRC ceiling, designated as "Bracket C".

As of January 1992, the contribution rates on Bracket B fall between an initial mandatory minimum rate of 4% by the employees and 8% by the employer for a total of 12%, to a maximum of 6% by the employees and 10% by the employer for a maximum of 16% rate of contribution. The minimum mandatory contribution rate to AGIRC on Bracket C is 8%. The *taux de cotisation* is negotiated between the employer and the *représentant du personnel* (employees' representatives).

Since January 1, 1991, a surcharge (*majoration*) of 17% of the above mentioned rates is added to the contributions; but there are no pension credits given for the surcharge.

Most employers have adopted the maximum rate of contribution on Bracket B. (The average rate of contribution on a national basis is over 14% on Bracket B salaries).

b. How to Calculate Your Retirement Benefits

This information is probably what you were hoping to learn by reading this section. The answer is: you cannot calculate your own retirement benefits unless you have access to actuarial tables, computers, and seven years of studies at the *Institut des Actuaires de France*. Because of the complexity of the system and the fact that the benefits under AGIRC are based on pension points purchased by a fixed rate of contribution that changes on an annual basis, it is difficult to convert pension points into a percentage-related salary (as the value of the French Franc in 1960, for example, is not the same as in 1993.)

Calculation of the points is also very difficult -almost impossible- because when a person changes jobs and the new employer is not affiliated with the same retirement association (*caisse*), his file goes to the new association and the number of points already accumulated is changed if the value of the points at the time of the change of jobs is not the same. In a career, there may be five or six changes of associations from which the final count goes to the ARRCO or AGIRC organization. Many different *caisses* are handled by the AGIRC. The same is true for ARRCO. These *caisses* will refer to AGIRC or ARRCO for the calculation and final computation of the points and value. However, both the AGIRC and the ARRCO *caisses*, as well as the CNAVTS, will prepare estimates of pension amounts beforehand. Such estimates are free. One can even request them a long time in advance to help with planning.

2. ARRCO--*Association des Régimes de Retraites Complémentaires*

In addition to AGIRC contributions, a contribution is mandatorily due on earnings up to the *Sécurité Sociale* ceiling (designated as Bracket A). However, this contribution, which amounts currently to 5% of Bracket A earnings, is not paid to an AGIRC pension foundation but to a non-*cadres* funding institution (*caisse de retraite*) affiliated with ARRCO. ARRCO groups a number of funding institutions which manage the pensions for the non-*cadres*. These funding institutions operate under the same rules.

VI. GENERAL OVERVIEW OF THE SYSTEM

Chart 2: Definition of Annual Salary Brackets (Figures as of January 1, 1993)

Salaries in France are divided into 4 Brackets:

- BRACKETS 1, 2, 3 and 4 or
- also known as "BRACKETS A, B, C and D"

Bracket C = FF 599,280-covers *cadres supérieurs* Bracket C is equal to 4 x Bracket A	Bracket C ceiling = A + B + C Brackets FF 1,198,560
Bracket B = FF 449,460-covers *cadres* and *agents de maîtrise* (foremen) Bracket B is equal to 3 x Bracket A	Bracket B ceiling = A + B Brackets FF 599,280
Bracket A = FF 149,820-covers everybody Part of salary between FF O and the *Sécurité Sociale* ceiling (the monthly ceiling changes each year on January 1st and July 1st.)	Annual *Sécurité Sociale* ceiling= FF 149,820

Chart 3: Scheme for Management Personnel (*les Cadres*)

AGIRC on Bracket C - Obligatory contribution as of 01/01/91 - Minimum 8% increased by 17% i.e. 8% x 17% = 1.36%; plus original 8% = 9.36% - Companies have the choice of the following contribution rates: - 8%-10%-12%-14%-16% And for companies created since 01/01/91: -12%-14%-16%
AGIRC on Bracket B - Obligatory contribution of 12% increased by 17% of that 12%, i.e., 14.04% Optional supplementary contribution of 2% or 4%: **Either** a rate of 14% increased by 17% of that 14% i.e., 16.38% **Or** a rate of 16% increased by 17% of that 16% i.e., 18.72%

ARRCO on Bracket A	*Sécurité Sociale*
Obligatory contribution of 4% increased by 25% i.e., 5% Optional supplementary contribution of 1% to 4% increased by 25%	Contribution of 14.75% on Bracket A plus 1.6% contribution on total salary (Brackets A, B & C). This contribution is paid jointly by employee and employer, usually 1/3 and 2/3.

Each retirement organization which is a member of AARCO and AGIRC has its own coefficient and way of calculating the number of points given under Brackets B and C.

You may have changed organizations 5 or 6 times during your career. Each time a re-evaluation is necessary.

Chart 4: Scheme for Non-Management Personnel (*non-cadres*):

<u>AGIRC</u>

- For *non-cadre* "Article 36" personnel, Bracket C is used or "GMP"
(GMP = *Garantie Minimum de Points*)
through an optional extension to the AGIRC management system
- Minimum rate of 12% increased by 17% of the 12%, i.e., 14.04%

Note: Although Article 36 personnel are not theoretically *cadre,*, they are treated like *cadre* at the time of retirement.

<u>ARRCO on Bracket B</u>

Bracket B is based on a salary which cannot exceed 3 times
the annual *Sécurité Sociale* ceiling.

Obligatory contribution: 4% increased by 25% of that 4%, i.e., 5%

Optional supplementary contribution:

- from 1% to 4% of Bracket A, increased by 25%
- from 1% to 12% on Bracket B, which cannot exceed 3 x the annual *Sécurité Sociale* ceiling, increased by 25%

or a maximum rate of 16% increased by 17% of that 16%, i.e., 18.72%

SECURITE SOCIALE OLD AGE PENSION CONTRIBUTION (*Assurance Vieillesse*)

This is compulsory when working in France.

14.75% of Bracket A ceiling
plus 1.60% of total salary

The same system is used for all Brackets.

Chart 5: ARRCO-AGIRC: The Rules

	Age 60	Between 60 &65	Age 65
Conditions to be met in order to be eligible to receive retirement benefits	1) Stop working 2) Contribute to the *Sécurité Sociale* old age scheme(s) for 37.5 years or 150 trimesters 3) Contribute to the *Sécurité Sociale* old age pension system	1) Stop working 2) Between 32,5 and 37,5 years of contributing 3) Contribution to the *Sécurité Sociale* old age pension system	1) Stop working 2) Contribute to the *Sécurité Sociale* old age scheme(s) for 37.5 years or 150 trimesters 3) Contribute to the *Sécurité Sociale* old age pension system
Amount of Pension	Pension = total points acquired each year x the value of the pension point at retirement date Points acquired per year = yearly contribution divided by the reference salary from ARRCO/AGIRC institutions **Full pension;** **(Application of a reduction factor if the contributory period is less than 37.5 years.)**	Pension = total points acquired each year x the value of the pension point at retirement date Points acquired per year = yearly contribution divided by the reference salary from ARRCO/AGIRC institutions **Application of a reduction factor if the contributory period is less than 37.5 years**	Pension = total points acquired each year x the value of the pension point at retirement date Points acquired per year = yearly contribution divided by the reference salary from ARRCO/AGIRC institutions **Full pension**

(continued on next page)

	Age 60	Between 60 & 65	Age 65
CONDITIONS TO BE FULFILLED FOR THE PENSION TO BE PAYABLE TO THE WIDOW/WIDOWER	Widow: age 50; Or immediately if: * an invalid * has 2 dependent children Widower usually age 60 or 65 according to the scheme or immediately if: * an invalid * has 2 dependent children AGIRC: no minimum duration of marriage (stipulated since 1/1/68) ARRCO: no minimum duration of marriage (stipulated since 1/1/80) The deceased spouse must have been affiliated with the supplementary schemes (whether he or she contributed or not). → **The reversion pension is cancelled in the event of remarriage.**		

VII. DETERMINING RETIREMENT BENEFITS

Understanding *Sécurité Sociale* and the ARRCO-AGIRC systems does not answer the question "How much will my retirement benefits be?"

Before attempting to answer this question, one must keep in mind that:

*No two retirement schemes are the same since benefits are determined by numerous factors which vary in each individual case. These factors are examined in detail in Section B below.

*It is impossible to give general estimates for self-employed persons (*profession libérale*) such as lawyers, doctors, freelance journalists, etc., or for those who own their own business. In these cases, an individual estimate has to be calculated. Consulting firms such as William M. Mercer-Faugère et Jutheau can prepare what is called an "individualized career reconstitution" to estimate the retirement benefits one can expect.

VIII. HOW TO MAXIMIZE RETIREMENT BENEFITS

The French *Sécurité Sociale* system is currently under severe strain. The number of unemployed and retired people receiving benefits has increased greatly. The work force is aging, and there is a depressed labor market.

This has resulted in increased taxation and contributions to fund the benefits for both the active and non-working populations.

The following brief explanation may help clarify what can be done on an individual basis if you have extra capital.

A. THE CAPITALIZATION SYSTEM AND INSURANCE
(*Système de Capitalisation*)

The capitalization system is based on the concept of individual long-term capital accumulation managed by financial institutions on a collective basis, i.e. under the form of specific mutual funds. Therefore the affiliation and contribution rates can be chosen. The payment of the pension is not linked to the payment of annuities (yearly payments until death) from the obligatory pension schemes: *Sécurité Sociale*, ARRCO, AGIRC.

The contribution rate chosen, either by a company or an individual, can be modified as desired. Each year, contributions made to a member's account increase his acquisition of rights (*droits*) within the plan. This increased acquisition is called "accrued pension rights" or *des droits individualisés*. At the end of each year, the amount (in FF) of the accrued pension rights is communicated by the insurer to the insured. This amount is guaranteed by the insurance company.

The increase in monetary value totaling 8-9% is based on two factors: the guaranteed minimum return rate (4.5% as of September 1992), and the supplementary valorization rate resulting from the financial investments (*taux de valorisation de l'épargne*).

The role of insurance in the capitalization system is to guarantee that the contributions paid to the insurance company will be transmitted to designated survivors in the case of the death of the insured.

Although the *répartition* and capitalization systems have similar goals, the means by which these two systems achieve their goals are different. High interest rates in the 1980's have made the two systems complementary.

A combination of the two systems is probably the ideal solution for both the company and the individual.

B. THE COMPANY: HOW IT CAN INCREASE THE LEVEL OF RETIREMENT BENEFITS FOR ITS EMPLOYEES

If you are working, you can ask the personnel director to tell you the number of points you have acquired since you joined the company. A consulting firm may provide you with a more accurate estimate of what your pension will be.

Retirement benefits are determined at two different levels: at the company level and at the individual level. The individual level will be dealt with in Section B below.

Supplementary insurance pension plans are now fairly common for top management and are being extended to the whole *cadre* category. In fact, an increasing number of company pension plans and retirement lump sums are financed on a pre-funded (*pré-financé*) basis; employers prefer this method of supplementing retirement benefits over making additional contributions...up to ARRCO-AGIRC limits...which they cannot control. Under the pre-funded pension plan, funds <u>must</u> be placed with an insurance company to be tax deductible.

As explained below, supplementary insurance pension plans may be implemented on either a set benefit or a set contribution basis.

1. Set Contribution Pension Plan (*Contrat Collectif de Retraite à Contributions Définies*)

A Set Contribution Pension Plan is a system by which the company pays a specific sum into a plan of an insurance company in order to finance a pension for employees. The contribution paid by the company is based on a fixed percentage of the total salaries paid during the year.

Each employee has an account with the insurance company. When the employee reaches retirement age, the accumulated capital is converted into a life annuity. The level of this annuity is known only when the retirement age is reached.

With a Set Contribution Pension Plan, the company knows the amount that is paid into the plan annually, but the pension is not guaranteed. It can only be estimated. The company is only obliged to pay a certain amount every year; no results are guaranteed.

a. Characteristics of the Set Contribution Pension Plan

* Contributions paid into the plan give a right to benefits to each employee.
* At retirement, accumulated capital can only be paid out in the form of an annuity or *rente viagère*.
* If the contract is cancelled, the acquired rights (money) still belong to the personnel insured before cancellation who continue to benefit from re-evaluations (i.e. interest rates). Money is paid in the form of annuities, according to the terms of the contract.

b. How the Set Contribution Pension Plan Operates

* Contributions paid are credited to the account of each employee.
* The member's account is credited with the interest by the insurer.
* Savings are transformed into life annuities by the insurer when the employee reaches retirement age.
* The benefits for each employee depend on the length of affiliation, the savings return rate, the total of contributions paid into each employee's account, and the age of the employee at retirement.

Tax consequences for contributions to the plan:

Contributions are deductible from net company operating income and are not considered taxable income for the employee when the following conditions are met:

* Benefits must be paid in the form of an annuity
* The pension is paid at the normal retirement date or, at the earliest, at age sixty
* The rates of contribution must be the same for each category of personnel
* There must be a collective agreement if the plan concerns a particular category of employee , or a unilateral decision from the employer if it concerns all personnel.

Tax consequences for benefits from the plan:
Retirement benefits are taxed in the same manner as personal income.

2. Set Benefit Pension Plan or Collective Pension Fund
(Contrat Collectif de Retraite à Prestations Définies)

Unlike the Set Contribution Pension Plan, the Set Benefit Pension Plan guarantees a specific percentage of financial earnings--for example, 75% of final earnings--including *Sécurité Sociale* and ARRCO-AGIRC benefits.

This type of contract is largely used in England and the United States where it is known as a Set (Fixed) Benefit Keogh. The plan is complex and places a financial burden on the company. In France, only large companies are interested in this kind of pension fund because of the tax deductions possible, and because the beneficiaries have high salaries and the company wishes to keep them in the company.

The Set (Fixed) Benefit Pension Plan offers large tax deductions and retirement benefits. However, it should be considered as a sophisticated system which requires expertise from an outside consulting firm and careful management on the part of the insurance company.

a. Characteristics of the Set (Fixed) Benefit Pension Plan

* The plan guarantees a fixed level of pension at the end of the career.

* In order to benefit from the supplementary pension, the employee must be working for the company at retirement date. If no longer with the company on the retirement date, the employee will not benefit from the contribution.

* The contract can be cancelled at any time. In this case, retirees continue to receive their pension, but those still working in the company lose future rights.

b. Operation of the plan

* The company establishes a fund managed by an insurance company to finance the pensions.
* The fund is built up by the payment of contributions.
* When an employee retires, the reserves (or accumulated capital) for the annuities to be paid are deducted from this fund.

Tax consequences: contributions are tax deductible from the company's taxable income only when benefits are paid in the form of pensions and not when paid in.

The funding mechanism: the level of the pension fund depends on the demography of the insured group, the salary distribution and growth rate, the financial performance of the organization managing the fund, and the rate of inflation.

C. THE INDIVIDUAL: HOW TO INCREASE THE LEVEL OF RETIREMENT BENEFITS

1. The insurance company as financial manager

Most people think first of banks when considering investment possibilities, unaware that insurance companies are important financial institutions in their own right, and offer a variety of investment possibilities.

While the role of a bank is to focus on short-term money management--managing checking accounts, offering means of payment such as credit cards and wire transfers, lending money through loans, and managing stock portfolios, --an insurance company, in fact, offers a broader range of long-term investment possibilities.

To understand the role of insurance in money management, it is important to distinguish between property/casualty insurance and life insurance.

Generally speaking, a property/casualty insurance carrier deals only with technical risks such as car, fire, civil liability, theft, etc. In exchange for a paid premium, the insurance company guarantees an indemnity for loss incurred. In France, property and casualty insurance is called *Incendie, Accidents et Risques Divers,* or *IARD.*

Life insurance differs in several ways from property and casualty insurance. Life insurance covers human risks and has two main purposes:
* to guarantee payment in case of a loss incurred by a person, and
* to protect investments by selecting long-term options according to the client's wish.

Unlike a bank, a life insurance carrier takes the risk of death and dismemberment into consideration, using mortality curves in calculating costs and benefits.

The following section details the different financial products available through insurance companies, explaining their role in maximizing retirement benefits and enhancing money management.

a. Insurance Products for Capitalization

1. Endowment Insurance (*Assurance en Cas de Vie*)

This type of contract is designed for capitalization only and not for protection against risk. The insured pays either a one-time premium or a periodical premium during a set period.

If the insured is alive at the end of the contract, he will receive either the capital or a life annuity from the insurance company. In case the insured dies before the expiration date, the capital is paid to the designated beneficiaries.

At the client's request, the premiums can be invested in different currencies such as French francs, US dollars, Japanese yen, British pounds, etc. This may be useful for those who have expenses in foreign countries, or who may retire outside of France.

The distinguishing factor of the endowment type of insurance contract is that an expiration date is set. This information can be useful to someone who knows precisely his or her date of retirement. Usually, endowment contracts are entered into by paying a single premium, superior to 50,000 FF, invested for a period of twenty years.

2. Save-as-You-Earn Plans (*Contrats à Versements Libres*)

Save-As-You-Earn Plans are the most common type of insurance capitalization product on the market. The client contributes the amount he wishes to his account as often as he wishes. No investment planning is made. A save-as-you-earn plan operates as an investment account to which sums can be deposited with no minimum or maximum required.

Premiums are usually invested in bonds or real estate. Interest earned is credited and consolidated annually. In most contracts, no capital loss is possible.

The guaranteed minimum return rate is 4.5%. In 1992, the savings return rate was approximately 8.5-9% per year.

In the event that the insured dies, acquired capital is paid to beneficiaries, tax-free. In order to be free of capital gains taxes, capitalization plans must be in effect at least 8 years before any money is withdrawn.

3. Individual Retirement Account (*Plan d'Epargne Populaire or PEP*)

The French version of the IRA was created in 1990 and can be held through banks or insurance companies. It is a tax scheme or *envelope fiscale avec des avantages fiscaux*. whose main characteristics are:
* In order to avoid capital gains taxes, money must be invested for more than eight years;
* Deposits can be made as frequently as the client wishes;
* The maximum amount for each contract is 600,000 FF (1,200,000 FF for a couple filing a joint tax return);
* Returns on investment are capitalized tax-free, that is , no taxes on the capital gains.
* 1 000 F (+ 250 F for each dependent child) may be deducted each year from income tax.

The PEP is an excellent product.

The difference between a "Bank PEP" and an "Insurance PEP"

An insurance PEP is above all an insurance contract, with all tax and estate advantages attached to it. In the case of a bank PEP, the accumulated capital is not paid to the beneficiaries upon the death of the client until inheritance taxes are paid. (Some banks offer a PEP which is indeed, an insurance PEP. Check with your bank.)

An insurance PEP is best suited for those who are mainly interested in an income tax-free life annuity. Furthermore, it may be the best product to improve the level of one's retirement benefits.

Only an insurance company can guarantee that capital accumulated at the term of the contract will be paid out in the form of a life annuity. In addition, money placed in an insurance PEP may be invested in various financial products such as foreign currencies, real estate shares, etc., whereas most bank PEP accounts rely solely on the bond markets.

4. *Plan d'Epargne en Actions (PEA)*
(a stock market-based savings plan)
In July 1992, a law was passed creating the *Plan d'Epargne en Actions*, or PEA. This step was taken by the French government to encourage people to invest in companies the French consider high-risk investments.

Investment in a PEA should be considered carefully for several reasons. It represents a risk similar to that of investing in the stock market: great gains may be made, but great losses may be suffered. Therefore, one should invest only a limited amount of money in a PEA, not the entire savings of an individual.

A PEA is not a life insurance contract. Therefore, in case of the death of the investor, the capital will not be transferred to the beneficiaries on a tax-free basis but will become part of the estate and be taxed.

Finally, it is fairly difficult to judge the performance of this kind of product on a long-term basis since it is one of the first of its kind to be introduced by financial institutions to date.

a. Characteristics of a PEA

A PEA can be opened by anyone paying income tax in France. It can be handled by a stock broker, an insurance broker, a bank, or the French post office (a very good financial management organization which Americans do not think of as managing money).

Just as with a PEP, the maximum amount of money which can be invested in a PEA is, for a married couple, 1,200,000 FF or, for an individual, 600,000FF. Only one PEA can be established per person or couple.

Once a PEA is established, contributions of the following sort may be made:
* shares of investment certificates of French companies traded on the French stock exchange
* shares of investment certificates purchased at the creation of a company
* shares of a SICAV (mutual fund) of which more than 60% is invested in stocks
* shares of an FCP (*Fonds Commun de Placement*, another type of mutual fund) of which more than 75% is invested in stocks.

French law requires that not more than 25% of the money invested in a PEA be used to purchase shares in one single company.

b. Tax Consequences and Benefits of the PEA

The main purpose of the PEA is to capitalize, without taxes, the returns on investment. Dividends, interest income and capital gains are tax exempt if the PEA has been in existence for five years or more.

After eight years, the owner of the PEA can choose between receiving the capital or a life annuity. As in the case of the life annuity generated by a PEP, the PEA life annuity is totally exempt from income tax for the investor.

c. Withdrawal of Money Before Term

Any sum withdrawn from the plan before the end of the eight-year term will automatically terminate the plan. Then, capital gains are taxed in the following manner:
* Before the end of the second year, capital gains are taxed at 24.6%.
* Between the third year and the end of the fifth year, capital gains are taxed at 18.1%, only if the volume of the shares sold during the year is in excess of 316,900 FF. (1992 figures)
* No taxes are due for capital gains on withdrawals made after five years.

d. Withdrawals After the Eight-Year Term

After the eight-year term, withdrawals can be made at any time, but no additional deposits are possible. This rule is designed to prevent investment in a PEA and obtaining capital gains without paying taxes.

5. Guaranteed Investment Contract (*Bon de Capitalisation*)

For those not interested in life annuity or the estate advantages of life insurance, another form of investment should be considered: the *Bon de Capitalisation*, or Guaranteed Investment Contract.

This type of contract is appropriate for the investor who has an "extra" sum of money that is not immediately needed. A low-risk investment, it offers a guaranteed rate and allows the owner to foresee the evolution of his estate with great precision. On the other hand, for these reasons, it does not offer particularly high interest and should not be the choice of the investor seeking a high return on investment.

Money paid on such a contract is invested in bonds or in mutual funds made up of bonds.

The main characteristic of a Guaranteed Investment Contract is that the interest rate is fixed for the entire length of the contract. This rate is usually between 6% and 9% per year. The minimum duration of such a contract is eight years. After eight years, no capital gains taxes have to be paid. During the first eight years, capital gains are heavily taxed (at 38% between 4 and 8 years).

The Guaranteed Investment Contract can be transferred to a beneficiary in case of the death of the policy holder, but that person will not benefit from the tax-free conditions. Since there may be no name on the contract, it can be given to anyone the investor chooses but that person will have to pay inheritance and capital gains taxes. (This enables a person to leave money anonymously to someone other than a spouse or children.)

6. Income-Producing Contract or Life Annuities (*Rentes Viagères*)

At retirement age, many people may have a sizeable estate but a relatively low income, partly because of the weaknesses of the various pension systems. It may be wise to transform some of their estate into income using a life annuity, or *rente viagère* which transforms a capital into a sum paid periodically. The amount is determined by the beneficiary's age.

In most cases, life annuities can be set up by the beneficiary who gives capital to a life insurance company. The company agrees to pay back this capital, plus interest accrued, on a quarterly or annual basis. However, the beneficiary must bear in mind that the ownership of the capital given is definitively transferred to the insurance company.

A life annuity contract may be implemented on an immediate or deferred basis. In the first case, the payment of the annuity starts as soon as the contract is established. In the second case, payment begins at a set date.

A life annuity contract can include a reversion clause under which the annuity will be transferred to the spouse on the death of the first beneficiary. Within certain limits, no inheritance taxes are paid on such a transfer.

Taxation of Life Annuities

Life annuity policy holders are obliged to declare amounts paid by the insurance company. However, only a portion of this amount will be taxed, depending on the age of the beneficiary:

Age of beneficiary	Percentage of annuity taxable
less than 50 years old	70%
50-59	50%
60-69	40%
over 70	30%

2. Conclusion concerning Insurance Products

It is important to keep in mind that a life annuity contract is irreversible: once the capital is turned over to the insurance company, it cannot be retrieved by the client. It is a way of protecting oneself and one's money from greedy children or from possible mental deterioration.

At the expiration of a PEP, the alternatives are
1) getting the capital in a lump sum, OR
2) having a life annuity paid by the insurer.

Some investors may prefer to keep control of the money, to manage it by themselves in order to take advantage of available tax shelters. The tax consequences of such a choice must be carefully considered.

→   **Once the choice is made, it cannot be changed.**

Life annuities guarantee great security. The insurance company is obliged to pay the annuity throughout the lifetime of the client. The main drawback is the inaccessibility of the capital. This problem can often be avoided thanks to the use of a computerized payment schedule known as the *Programmation de retraits partiel* which is made on a life insurance contract.

With the plan for partial withdrawals (*programmation de retraits partiels*), the insurance company calculates and programs yearly or quarterly payments of a defined percentage of the amount invested in a life insurance contract.

Chart 6: Summary of Lump Sum, Life Annuity and *Programmation de Retraits Partiels*

	ADVANTAGES	DISADVANTAGES
1) Lump sum	Tax-free and you manage it for tax shelters, etc.	None, but you have to know how to manage your money.
2) Life Annuity	Tax-free when obtained through a PEP . No worries. You know what you'll get each month until you die and no one can make you sign away your money.	If you happen to die a month later, your family receives nothing. The insurance company keeps remaining assets.
3)*Programmation de retraits partiels*	You can still get at your money while receiving regular income. After eight years, no tax.	During first eight years, money withdrawn is taxable.

IX. DEATH, INSURANCE AND THE ESTATE

As we have seen, insurance can be an excellent means by which to increase the level of retirement benefits. It is also an excellent tool for people who are planning to leave their estate to heirs when they die.

In this respect, under certain conditions, life insurance permits leaving some money to an heir free of inheritance taxes.

How are estates taxed in France? (See also "Wills and Inheritance in France" by Persis Gouirand.)

Taxation rates and conditions vary dramatically depending on individual circumstances. Now we will consider direct-line inheritance, or inheritance from parents to children, using the new inheritance taxation rates.

The first 330,000FF for spouses is inherited tax-free. Direct descendants and ascendants are accorded an initial deduction of 300,000FF.

Anything above 300,000FF will be taxed as follows:

Chart 7: Inheritance Taxes (Direct Descendants and Ascendants)

Taxable part	Tax rate applicable
0-50,000FF	5%
50,000-75,000	10%
75,000-100,000	15%
100,000-3,400,000	20%
3,400,000-5,600,000	30%
5,600,000-11,200,000	35%
above 11,200,000	40%

For the surviving spouse, anything above 330,000FF will be taxed as follows:

Inheritance Taxes (Surviving Spouse)

Taxable part	Tax rate applicable
0-50,000FF	5%
50,000-100,000	10%
100,000-200,000	15%
200,000-3,400,000	20%
3,400,000-5,600,000	30%
5,600,000-11,200,000	35%
above 11,200,000	40%

Rates are higher for brothers, sisters and collaterals; in the case of relatives beyond the fourth degree and non-relatives, the rates go up to 60%.

It is important to note that life insurance such as a PEP or "save-as-you-earn" plan will decrease inheritance taxes only if the age of the insured at subscription date is less than seventy years and only on the money invested before age seventy. Afterwards, life insurance loses its advantage as a tax-shelter, and no additional money should be invested.

Anyone seeking to reduce inheritance taxes via an insurance product should bear in mind that only 25% of an estate can be invested in insurance. Failure to observe this limit can bring on legal prosecution.

In conclusion, the use of life insurance to reduce inheritance taxes must be considered carefully. The choice of such a scheme should only be made after a thorough analysis of the situation of each person planning to leave money to his or her heirs.

It is also very important that couples married for 25-30 years be under the *Communauté Universelle* marriage contract in order to be protected after the death of one partner against the greed of children or children's spouses (whom the French call *les pièces rapportées*). Again, see "Wills and Inheritance in France" by Persis Gouirand to find out more about the *Communauté Universelle*.

X. CONCLUSION

The information in this section was compiled in an effort to explain the complex topic of retirement schemes in France. Given the difficult economic climate and France's aging *Sécurité Sociale* system, understanding the private and supplementary retirement schemes available is of increasing importance to those who plan to work and retire in France.

An additional objective was to provide a clear understanding of the role of insurance in supplementary retirement benefits and to provide an explanation of the major life insurance products available today.

Even the most standard cases can benefit from the expertise offered by a consultant specialised in retirement benefits. Investment made in a personalized analysis by such a consultant may help to secure and maximize retirement benefits.

Benoit Besson
February 1993

WILLS AND INHERITANCE
in France

Prévenir n'est pas mourir

by Persis GOUIRAND

WILLS AND INHERITANCE

by Persis Gouirand

TABLE OF CONTENTS

ABOUT THE AUTHOR

Persis Gouirand, a graduate of Wheaton College in Massachusetts, received her Masters from the Middlebury College Graduate School of French in France. She is married to Jean-Pierre Gouirand and is the mother of three children.

Having lived in France for twenty-five years, she is now a partner with two other AAWE members of At Home Abroad, an executive relocation company whose business is introducing other foreigners to Paris.

Persis joined AAWE in 1978 and has volunteered her skills in various capacities including several years as editor of the AAWE newsletter.

ACKNOWLEDGEMENT

AAWE and the author of this guide gratefully acknowledge the invaluable assistance provided by **Samuel Okoshken, Esq.**, a partner in the Paris-based American law firm of Levine & Okoshken.

PREVENIR N'EST PAS MOURIR

FOREWORD

The writing of this guide--which turned out to be a much more ambitious project than I had originally bargained for--was inspired by my admiration for the AAWE Guide to Education and the consequent desire to contribute to the continuation of this public service; co-incidentally, the untimely deaths, in fairly close succession, of three members of my French husband's family opened my eyes to the significant differences between French and American laws dealing not only with inheritance, but with property in general.

The most striking revelation was that you are not free to do as you please with your own property, and that in one sense you do not really possess what you may have thought was unquestionably yours. Whereas in some countries it is possible to write your closest relatives out of your will and leave your entire fortune to the proverbial cats' home, this is not so in France.

In the process of my research, through which I hoped to gain knowledge which would be useful to me personally as well as to the readers of the guide, I came to the realization that, in spite of my twenty-odd years of residence in this country, there are still aspects of French culture that had escaped my notice.

A bit of historical background on the current laws and attitudes

Before the Revolution, French inheritance laws were based on the double tradition of codified, Roman law and unwritten, common law. The former gave full power to an individual over his property; the latter subscribed to the feudal principle of keeping possessions, especially land in the family, and favoring the eldest son by leaving him the bulk of the family property.

In an excess of egalitarian zeal, the Revolution put an end to this by decreeing that nine-tenths of a deceased person's property would be divided among all surviving relatives, according to a complex and rigid system of apportionment. This of course resulted in the fractioning of estates and endless disputes. It did, however, do much to further the Revolution's political goal of reforming society along egalitarian lines.

Napoleon's Civil Code, which he called a mass of granite, made the personal lives of citizens a state concern by viewing marriage as a contract. Napoleon, a notorious anti-feminist, was convinced that social order depended on the subjugation of wives to their husbands. Article 1428 made the husband the administrator of his wife's wealth. He also tended to favor blood lines over marriage ties. His code presupposes that people related by blood are emotionally closer than those linked by matrimony, which, thanks to the Code, was no longer necessarily "holy".

The Civil Code retained the Revolutionary principle of rejection of the feudal system; its laws, however, are based on the Roman legal premise that a property owner is master of his possessions. It nevertheless imposes on the testator certain obligations vis à vis members of his immediate family, both parents and children.

Thus the established rule incorporated both the former common law, which held that goods must be left only to blood relatives (excluding the spouse), and the former codified law, which was based on the notion that one may dispose of possessions as one sees fit.

* * * * *

This background explains why current French law includes the principle of forced heirship, according to which it is impossible to disinherit a child. At the same time, it allows for some leeway through what is called the *quotité disponible* which can be willed to whomever one wishes. Unfortunately, especially for couples with even one child, this discretionary portion rarely amounts to more than half (and usually less) since it is only this available remainder which can legally be left to one's spouse. The latter often finds her standard of living significantly reduced upon the death of her husband. (It is interesting to note that some American states also have forced heirship laws...in favor of the surviving spouse!)

In times when life expectancy was much shorter it was not uncommon for a parent to die while children were still small and therefore needful of legal protection against the consequences of a possible remarriage of the surviving parent. People live much longer today, and usually children have become self-sufficient adults by the time one of their parents passes away. The surviving parent is often an elderly widow with a modest income.

It should be pointed out that, like many French tradition-bound institutions, inheritance laws do not necessarily reflect the current attitude of the French population. While many parents still consider the transmission of property as their supreme duty, most prefer, as do Americans, to give their children the best possible education, rather than just endowing them with capital. They want their savings to go to their spouse, and many deplore the system which prevents them from ensuring that this will happen. But, like many other institutions, this one is slowly evolving towards a recognition of present reality: a recent bill * introduced in the *Conseil des Ministres* takes into account, and considerably ameliorates, the plight of the surviving spouse whose husband dies intestate.

This legislation is still only pending, however, and it is not known when it will actually become law. We hope that this guide will encourage you to do everything possible within the framework of the existing law to ensure your future financial security and your present peace of mind.

Persis W. Gouirand

* *Projet de Loi No. 2530 Relatif aux Droits des Héritiers;* for more information on the current status of this proposed legislation, call the *Journal Officiel*, tel: 40.58.75.00. or tel: 40.58.76.00. Their Minitel service is 36.16 code JOEL.

INTRODUCTION

As an American residing in France, your first encounter with French inheritance laws may come as a surprise--and not necessarily a pleasant one. In contrast to American legislation, you have much less latitude to dispose of your property as you see fit, and at least part of your estate will be apportioned according to a set of precise rules. IF YOU ARE LEGALLY DEEMED TO BE DOMICILED IN FRANCE WHEN YOU DIE, FRENCH INHERITANCE LAWS WILL APPLY. THE FORCED HEIRSHIP RULES WILL NORMALLY OVERRULE ANY CONTRARY PROVISION IN YOUR WILL.

The principle that governs the forced heirship rules is that worldly possessions should be passed along blood lines, keeping family wealth in the family and out of the hands of intruders, such as daughters- and sons-in-law. Indeed, French law makes it impossible to disinherit a direct descendant (unless it has been proven that he has attempted to murder you!), thus protecting children whose mother or father remarries. There will always be a part of their parent's estate which is reserved for them and them alone.

This reserved portion of an estate is in fact called *la réserve*, and those who are entitled to it are known as *héritiers réservataires*. They include descendants (children, grandchildren, great-grandchildren), parents, siblings, grandparents and great-grandparents, in that order. All other blood relatives, however, are superceded by the surviving spouse. A more detailed description of this hierarchy is given in Appendix 1.

The part of one's estate that can be freely disposed of, once the *héritiers réservataires* have been provided for, is called the *quotité disponible*. It is possible to bequeath the totality of this remainder to whomever one wishes. The *quotité disponible* is determined as a percentage of the deceased's total assets. The percentage varies according to the number of children of the deceased.

In this booklet, we will examine ways of maximizing one's disposable assets and providing as much protection as possible for one's spouse. First, however, let's see what happens when no precautions have been taken prior to death.

CHAPTER 1

Absence of any Will or Antenuptial Agreement -- Effect on the Surviving Spouse

French law does not consider the surviving spouse as a privileged heir. In other words, he/she is not an *héritier réservataire* (survivor who automatically inherits a portion of *la réserve*).

If the deceased has left no will or *donation* (lifetime gift), the surviving spouse must share the estate with the blood relatives of the deceased. According to their degree of kinship to the deceased, the surviving spouse may inherit full title (*pleine propriété*) to all or part of the estate, and/or life-interest (*l'usufruit*) of all or part of the estate.

Pleine propriété means both ownership and use of the inherited property. The *pleine propriétaire* possesses both the *nue-propriété* (ownership) and *l'usufruit*, and is therefore free to sell, rent, occupy, demolish or give away the property.

L'usufruit is the right during one's lifetime to benefit from a property (occupy it, use it, lease it and collect the rent) that belongs to someone else (who is said to have the *nue-propriété*). *L'usufruit* ceases automatically upon the death of the *usufruitier* (holder of the life-interest). The property cannot be sold by the *usufruitier* without written consent of the owner (the *nue-propriétaire*).

The surviving spouse inherits *pleine propriété* if there are no surviving *héritiers réservataires*. In such case, the spouse inherits full title to the entire estate. This, of course, is rare. (See chart, p.174).

If, in addition to his/her spouse (and possibly non-*réservataire* relatives), the deceased is survived by ancestors solely on the maternal or solely on the paternal side, the spouse is then entitled to the legal share which would have gone to the ancestors on the other side, had they still been alive. In other words, he/she inherits full title to half the estate, the other half going to the surviving *réservataire* relatives (the ancestors).

What happens if the deceased is survived by adulterine children (offspring of the deceased and a man or woman other than his/her spouse)? As descendants, these children have priority; but in this case the law provides for half of the estate to go to the wronged spouse.

The surviving spouse will therefore come into full title to half of the estate if the only survivors are him/herself and the adulterine children; whereas he/she will get full title to only a quarter of the property if there is also a surviving ancestor. In such a case, by virtue of their priority, the children will inherit three quarters of the estate, but the ancestor will receive nothing. The sole fact of his existence reduces the surviving spouse's portion and increases that of the adulterine children, but does not benefit the ancestor himself.

The surviving spouse inherits a life interest in <u>one quarter</u> of the deceased's property if the deceased is survived by any children or grandchildren (illegitimate, legitimate or adopted). As a rule of thumb, this may be thought of as equal to a bequest of 10% of the estate.

N.B. If there is discord between the descendants (who may be the offspring of a previous marriage) and the spouse, the position of the latter may be precarious. For instance, he/she may find himself/herself forced to leave the conjugal home if it belonged solely to the deceased. This in itself is sufficient reason for rushing out to make a will.

However, as this Guide was going to press, a bill was introduced in the *Conseil des Ministres* which, if adopted (which it is very likely), would modify the *Code Civil* as follows:

In the absence of any will, and assuming that the deceased left descendants, the surviving spouse will have the right to choose between life interest in the entire estate or full ownership of one-quarter of the estate. This is obviously a better deal than the previous life interest in only one-quarter.

Moreover, even if the deceased has expressly disinherited his/her spouse, the heirs are obliged to support him/her in the same style as before their benefactor's death, and in particular allow him/her to stay in the home for the rest of his/her life.

In the same bill, the successoral rights of adulterine children become identical to those of legitimate children.

If the deceased leaves no children of the marriage but is survived by:
    a. ancestors on both sides and/or
    b. siblings (or their descendants) and/or adulterine children
-- the surviving spouse will inherit a life interest in one half of the estate.

More details regarding the rules applying to a life interest are given in Appendix 2.

Having given you the bad news, we will now examine what steps can be taken before death to offset some of the injustices inherent in the French system and ensure that one's spouse -- or oneself -- is not left out in the cold.

CHAPTER 2

How to Ensure Maximum Protection for You and Your Spouse

There are three principal ways of ensuring that at least part of your assets end up in the right hands:

1. The choice of a marriage contract
2. The making of a will
3. Lifetime gifts

1.   *LES REGIMES MATRIMONIAUX*

Your marriage contract (*régime matrimonial*) determines how your estate will be divided.

By marrying, two people agree to share the use and sometimes the ownership of certain goods. When one partner dies, what happens under French law to the goods which he already possessed before marrying, and to those he acquired during the marriage? It all depends on what type of contract was chosen by the spouses. (The preceding section dealt with the situation when there was neither a will nor a marriage contract.) A marriage contract in France is made by a *notaire*.

What if no contract was made?

In this case, French law provides for a *régime légal* which applies automatically. This set of regulations was modified in 1966, with the result that those couples married in France prior to February 1, 1966 are subject to a different *régime* from those married after that date.

Those who celebrated their marriage before February 1, 1966 are considered to be married under a legal community (*communauté légale*) contract. This means that all personal property (furniture, cars, works of art, securities, business holdings, cash) is jointly owned, including that which belonged to each spouse before the wedding, and also including any goods received during the course of the marriage.

The one exception to this rule concerns real property (land and/or buildings), which remains the sole property of the spouse who originally owned it or who came into it by gift or inheritance during the marriage. Any real estate acquired jointly by the spouses of course remains common property.

Thus, a surviving spouse of such a marriage automatically retains half of all of the couple's jointly-owned property. The other half then is considered the deceased's estate and becomes subject to the previously-described rules governing inheritance.

If you were married in France after February 1, 1966 without a marriage contract, your *régime legal* is that of *la communauté des biens réduite aux acquêts*: marriage settlement through which only acquisitions (property acquired by the spouses) are considered jointly-owned. Contrary to the *communauté légale* contract, goods owned by each partner before the wedding, or acquired during the marriage through gift or inheritance, remain her sole property.

Everything else belongs to the couple, no matter whose money actually paid for it. Thus, when one partner dies, the other automatically keeps one half of their common property. The deceased's half becomes part of his estate, as does all of his personal, solely-owned property.

At the time of death, therefore, the couple's goods are first divided as follows:
- the surviving spouse retains full title to whatever was his/her personal property;
- the personal property of the deceased goes into the estate;
- the jointly-owned property is halved, one half going into the estate, the other half to the surviving spouse.

This is where things may get complicated, for not all goods (a house, for example), are easily divisible. The couple may have jointly financed improvements on a piece of property which actually belonged to only one of them, or the couple may have built a house on land which was willed to only one partner. Or this solely-owned land may have been sold to pay for a new home occupied, of course, by both partners.

It is up to the *notaire*, who enters the picture at death, to find and propose to the family an equitable formula for applying the terms of the marriage contract. Once the value of various goods has been assessed, he must calculate how either to compensate the estate by deducting something from the surviving spouse's share (a process called *récompense*) or to compensate the spouse from the estate (this is called *reprise*), depending on which share would otherwise be compromised

If, during the marriage, a piece of property was bought using funds received by one of the spouses through gift or inheritance, but there is no written record of this operation, then the property will probably be considered jointly-owned. However, if it can be proven that separate funds were used for this purchase, then the property will be considered as solely owned by that spouse, and will either be retained as personal property (in the case of a surviving spouse), or become part of the estate (if the purchaser was the deceased spouse). Therefore, if you wish to make clear that a piece of property was in fact paid for by you and only you, it should be stipulated in the notarized deed (*Acte de Vente*). The same precaution applies if a solely-owned piece of property is sold to finance the purchase of commonly-owned property. The amount of the personal investment must be clearly stated in the deed, in a clause known as the *clause de remploi*.

What are the various marriage contracts?

When you establish a notarized marriage contract, you must decide how your assets will be disposed of in case of divorce or death. In addition to the possibilities described above, there are several other types of contracts from which to choose. If you opt for *le régime de séparation des biens*, you exclude all possibility of commonly-held property. Everything, whether purchased or inherited, is labeled his or hers. To substantiate this separate ownership, it is a good idea to make sure your name is mentioned clearly on the proof of purchase. Goods acquired jointly are not common property; each spouse owns one-half.

The advantage of this system is that each spouse is responsible only for his own debts and cannot be held liable for those of his partner. For this reason, it is often chosen by business owners in order to protect their spouses in case of bankruptcy. The disadvantages of this system are many. If there is no proof of ownership of a specific piece of property (due to misplaced bills or checkstubs, etc.), the deceased's heirs can challenge the surviving spouse's ownership and the property can be considered as having belonged to both spouses. Thus, it is possible that, in spite of the name given to this system (*séparation des biens*), there will be a body of commonly-owned goods consisting of those that were jointly acquired (*biens indivis*) and those whose ownership is unclear or disputed. Half of these will become part of the estate and therefore the surviving spouse will be entitled to only half of what he/she may have thought he/she rightfully owned. In this case, the *notaire* can help to resolve conflicts by introducing clauses of *présomption de propriété*--presumption of ownership--into the marriage contract.

Also, unless the deceased has provided otherwise in his will, and assuming that there are children, the surviving spouse will inherit only the *usufruit* of only one quarter of the deceased's separate property. Unless the surviving spouse is independently well-off, she may find herself destitute.

La communauté universelle (residuary community) is recommended for couples who marry late in life and have no children. All of their goods, whatever their origins, will be considered as jointly-owned property. Therefore, when one spouse dies, there is no need to liquidate the marriage contract, for all the deceased's holdings will automatically go to the surviving spouse. If children are born later on, they will not be disinherited by virtue of such contract, but will simply have to wait for the second parent to die before claiming their inheritance. This is the system that most closely resembles the American practice of having all of the deceased's estate go to the surviving spouse who then passes it on to their children at her death.

Le régime de participation aux acquêts (system of sharing of acquired goods) is a compromise between the *régime de separation de biens* and the *régime de la communauté*. During the marriage, this system works exactly like the separate ownership contract, each spouse being the sole owner of his personal property. If the marriage is dissolved, it becomes a *régime de communauté*. This enables the partners to keep their patrimony and at the same time profit from any appreciation of value which has accrued during the marriage. This added value (or decreased value, as the case may be) is determined by comparing the worth of each spouse's holdings as assessed at the beginning and at the end of the union. If there has been a gain, each spouse is entitled to half the increase. (The marriage contract may provide for an unequal apportioning, e.g. 3/4 - 1/4 or 1/3 - 2/3.) If the final holdings of one of the spouses is inferior to its original value, the deficit is partially sustained by the other.

This system is supposed to combine the advantages of *communauté* and *séparation des biens* (for example, the spouse of a bankrupt business owner would not be responsible for his/her debts during the marriage but would benefit from the advantages of common ownership if things had been going well).

However, it is very difficult to implement, due to problems inherent in the assessment of the value of property. What often results is a protracted settlement fraught with conflict.

Clauses which may be included in the marriage contract

A clause of *attribution de communauté* (cognizance of community) or *partage inégal de la communauté* (unequal division of community property) can be included in a marriage contract. It stipulates that a specified part (2/3, 3/4) of commonly-owned property will belong to the surviving spouse, only the remainder being considered part of the estate, to be divided amongst the other heirs. This clause would affect debts in the same proportion as the attribution of property ownership. For example, if the contract attributed 3/4 to the deceased and 1/4 to the surviving spouse, then the latter must bear 1/4 of any debts of the deceased.

The insertion of this clause in a marriage contract is a good way of protecting the interests of one's spouse without totally excluding the other heirs. It can provide for either full ownership or simply a life interest (*usufruit*) and, not being considered a bequest, is not subject to inheritance tax at the death of the first spouse. The only thing to watch out for, however, is the possible existence of debts!

A clause known as *préciput* can be inserted in a *régime de communauté* contract. Under such provision, the couple can decide that a specific item of property or sum of money will automatically go to the surviving spouse before any division of the rest of the couple's holdings. This means that, in addition to half of the couple's belongings, the surviving spouse will have full title to, for instance, their home. Here again, this arrangement is not considered a bequest and is not subject to inheritance taxes until the death of the second spouse. **It is important to note that this clause must be inserted into a marriage contract before the wedding; afterwards it will be too late.**

Another possibility for modifying one's marriage contract to fit individual requirements is the *clause de prélèvement moyennant indemnité*. This clause stipulates that the surviving spouse can keep for herself certain goods (e.g. the conjugal home and the furniture contained therein) on condition that the other heirs are compensated in cash for the value of said goods. Thus, the other heirs cannot compel the surviving spouse to sell these goods in order to fund their share of the estate; the surviving spouse has a grace period of three to five years before having to pay the indemnity.

A *donation entre époux* (lifetime gift between spouses) can be included in the marriage contract and can include any kind of gift of both present and future goods. Unlike a *donation au dernier vivant* (see p.172), it is not revocable, even in the case of divorce.

Is it possible to change an existing marriage contract?

The answer is yes, on the condition that you have been married for at least two years. Whether you change completely (say, from *séparation de biens* to *communauté universelle*), or simply modify your old contract, it must be done officially by a *notaire* and a lawyer, who will request official confirmation of the contract from the *tribunal d'instance* (court of appeals) of the district where the couple lives. The judge of the appeals court will give his stamp of approval only after making sure that these modifications do not compromise the inheritance of any children involved. If there are minor children, such approval is normally refused.

It should be borne in mind that this procedure is fairly long (it takes from three to six months) and costly; in addition to the legal fees, charges related to the establishment of the contract start at FF2,000 and can amount to much more, depending on the assessed value of the patrimony involved. This is in addition to a tax of .6% for *publicité foncière* on the value of any real estate owned by either spouse.

It can, however, be advantageous to elderly childless couples who wish to go from a *communauté légale* or a *communauté réduite aux acquêts* to a *communauté universelle* (stipulating that all of the couple's possessions, whether individually or jointly owned, would go to the surviving spouse). This modification would eliminate inheritance taxes until the second death.

2. MAKING A WILL

It is clear from the preceding discussion that one should avoid intestacy at all costs. French law allows for the following choices to be offered by the terms of a will to the surviving spouse:

1. *Usufruit* of the entire estate;

2. Outright ownership of the entire *quotité disponible;* (The amount will vary according to the *héréditaires réservataires.*)

3. Regardless of the *quotité disponible*, outright ownership of 25% of the estate and life interest in the remainder.

The *donation entre époux* is also appropriate if one wishes to transmit the whole of one's *quotité disponible* to one's spouse; whereas a will is necessary if one desires to divide it among more than one survivor. By naming one's spouse the *légataire universelle* (residual legatee, i.e. the person who will be entitled to the maximum allowed by law once the *réserve* has been deducted), the spouse will inherit 100% of the *quotité disponible*.

How to Make a Will

The Holographic Will

Anyone can make a will at any time, in any place, simply by sitting down and putting on paper, preferably in indelible ink, the way in which he wishes his possessions to be distributed among his heirs. He can also deal with matters unrelated to his earthly possessions: how he wishes his body to be disposed of, how his funeral should be conducted; who should be appointed to take care of underage children, etc. There is no need for any witness or for the services of a French *notaire*. This kind of will is called a holographic will (*testament olographe*).

However, in order for this type of will to be valid, certain rules must be observed:

The will must be handwritten by the testator (*testateur*), signed, and clearly dated. If more than one page is needed, each page must be numbered, dated, and signed. If any of these requirements are not fulfilled, the will is automatically null and void.

If you wish to make a holographic will, it is wise to consult a *notaire* who will advise you, free of charge, as to the conformity of your document with legal requirements. He may even make suggestions as to the wording, although you are free to use whatever terms you choose. Then, if you so desire, you can leave it with him for safekeeping. You can, of course, keep copies in other places. You can even ask the *notaire* to register its existence (not its contents) on a centralized file for all of France. The fee for these services is less than 200FF per will.

The Notarized Will

It is also possible to make a notarized will (*testament authentique*), in the presence of one *notaire* and two witnesses or of two *notaires*, all of whom must be adult French nationals unrelated to the testator by blood or marriage.

It is the *notaire* who actually writes the documents on the instructions of the testator, whose wishes (but not necessarily his exact words) must be faithfully reproduced. The will is then read aloud and signed, after which it is consigned to the *notaire*'s archives for safekeeping.

A *testament authentique* is harder to contest than a holographic will, and there is no danger of its being declared void because of non-conformity. It is, however, more than twice as expensive and much less private in character.

The Secret Will

A secret will (*testament mystique ou secret*) is written, typed, or dictated, then signed by the testator. It is then put into a closed envelope which is sealed in front of a *notaire* and two witnesses. The *notaire* then draws up a document certifying that the testator has officially entrusted his will to him.

While a will can be modified by adding codicils (*codicilles*), or riders, it is considered better, for clarity's sake, to re-write the document entirely, specifying in the new will that its provisions supercede all previous wills.

A will can be made by only one person; there is no such thing as a joint will.

3.   LIFETIME GIFTS

It is possible to transfer the ownership of goods from one person to another while both are still alive. Here again, we find that French legislation has left nothing to chance, for there are extensive regulations governing this procedure. We will look at only those which have to do with gifts and other transfers between spouses; information regarding other types of *donation* may be found in Appendix 3.

Donation au dernier vivant

This is a special kind of lifetime transfer which can be made by one or both spouses to the other one. The main differences between this type of gift and those described in Appendix 3 are:

1. It is revocable.

2. It applies to all assets, present and future.
3. It does not come into effect until one of the spouses dies.
4. It is not automatically revoked at the birth of a child.

Each spouse can choose to give full ownership and/or life interest in all or part of his disposable assets; the only (!) restriction is that full title to any property not exceed the *quotité disponible spéciale*, i.e. the portion with which the spouse is entitled to do as he/she pleases. While *la réserve* can be bequeathed as *usufruit*, it must revert to the *héritiers réservataires* upon the death of the second spouse.

Obviously, the fact that this type of bequest is revocable simplifies matters in case of divorce. On the other hand, either spouse is perfectly free to cancel his/her gift without telling the other, which could cause the latter to be in for a disagreeable surprise!

Since this type of transfer includes both present and future assets, any applicable taxes are payable upon the death of the first spouse, not before. The notorial fee for drawing up the *Acte de Donation* is about 700FF.

INHERITANCE CHART

The following chart applies to all couples whatever their marriage contract.

Remember, though, that if the *régime* is one of *communauté*, the surviving spouse automatically keeps one-half of the couple's property (which doesn't even enter into the estate), and **therefore this chart illustrates what happens to the other half**.

In the case of a *séparation* contract, of course, **all of the deceased's belongings are divided as below**. This chart does NOT take into account pending French legislation as described in the framed text in CHAPTER 1.

The deceased is survived by the following heirs:	French law says they must receive:	This leaves a *quotité disponible* of:	The surviving spouse can inherit with **NO** will nor *donation entre vifs:*	The surviving spouse can inherit **WITH** will or *donation entre vifs:*
1 child	1/2 of his estate	the other half	life interest in 1/4	1) full ownership of 1/4 and life interest in 3/4 OR 2) life-interest in the entire estate OR 3) full ownership of 1/2
2 children	2/3 of his estate	the other third	idem	1) or 2) above OR full ownership of 1/3
3 children	3/4 of his estate	the other quarter	idem	1) or 2)above OR full ownership of 1/4
only grandchildren	1/2 of his estate = the portion which would have gone to their late parent	same as for one child		
both parents only	1/4 each (=1/2)	the other half	life-interest in 1/2	full ownership of 1/2 and simple ownership of 1/2
one parent only	1/4 of his estate	the other 3/4	full ownership of 1/2	full ownership of 3/4 and simple ownership of 1/4
grandparents	idem	idem	idem	idem
siblings and/or their offspring	whatever he chooses	whatever he chooses	life-interest in 1/2	the entire estate
other relatives	idem	idem	the entire estate	idem

full ownership = *pleine propriété*
life-interest = *usufruit*
simple ownership = *nue-propriété*

CHAPTER 3

Life Insurance

Life insurance may be the only legal and uncomplicated way to circumvent the French forced heirship laws. The advantage of a life insurance policy is that the policy-owner may choose the beneficiary. Since life insurance is not considered as part of the estate, it is not subject to either inheritance laws or taxes. In case of a couple whose marriage contract is that of *communauté réduite aux acquêts*, for example, the sum paid to the surviving spouse by the insurance company is not considered part of the community property.

While certain measures have been taken to limit the amount of capital which can be exempted from estate taxes (e.g. in the case of an elderly person taking out an insurance policy for the first time), life insurance, which in some other countries is subject to tax, is considered in France to be the only legal way to avoid paying inheritance taxes.

There are many good reasons to take out a life insurance policy: to protect a surviving spouse who has no other source of income; to guarantee that one's offspring will be able to continue their education, to ensure the ongoing care of a handicapped child. It is even possible to insert a clause specifying that the capital be used to pay any inheritance taxes, thus sparing one's heirs this financial burden.

In France, there is a variety of contracts from which to choose. The main thing is to deal with a reputable life insurance company and an agent you trust. We emphasize this point due to the proliferation of unscrupulous agents (*courtiers*) who prey on the unsuspecting. If a door-to-door salesman tries to induce you to sign a policy, don't give in. If you do regret signing a paper, remember that you have eight days in which to change your mind, although apparently it is not always easy to get in touch with these salesmen once they have absconded with your check.

The cost of an insurance policy varies according to the type of insurance, the age of the policyholder, and the amount of capital insured.

The various kinds of contracts include:

Assurance temporaire (temporary insurance) or *à fonds perdu* (annuity).
The insurer pays a capital to the beneficiary only if the insured person dies during the duration of the contract. If the policyholder is still alive when it comes to term, he is owed nothing, unless he has also taken out a special policy providing for the reimbursement of premiums paid by him.

Assurance vie entière (full life insurance)
In this case, the insurance company pays the capital to the beneficiary upon the death of the policyholder, no matter what the date. This contract is more expensive that the temporary insurance policy. The older the policyholder at the time he takes out the policy, the higher the premiums.

Assurance mixte (composite insurance)

The insurance company pays a capital either at the end of the term of the contract, or at the death of the policyholder, whichever occurs first. This type of policy is also expensive.

Rente éducation (education annuity)

This is a stipend paid to school-age children until they become adults or finish their studies.

Rente de conjoint (spouse's annuity)

This stipend is paid to the surviving spouse until his or her death or until the beginning of a *pension de réversion* (see Appendix 4).

It should be noted that American life insurance can also accomplish most of the objectives described above.

For more information on French life insurance policies, contact:

--Institut National de la Consommation, 80 rue Lecourbe, 75015 Paris;
Tel: 45.66.20.20.
--Centre de Documentation et d'Information de l'Assurance, 2, rue de la Chaussée d'Antin, 75009 Paris; Tel: 42.46.13.13.
--Federation Française des Sociétés d'Assurance, 26, boulevard Haussmann, 75009 Paris;
Tel: 42.47.90.00.

CHAPTER 4

Special Considerations Affecting Americans Living in France

It has already been pointed out in this booklet that French inheritance laws will automatically apply to the estate of anyone who is domiciled in France at the time of death. While there are exceptions to this rule, most of us whose spouses are French will be affected by these laws.

Determining your *régime de mariage*

The first thing to do when planning or settling an estate in France is to determine one's *régime de mariage*. If you were married in France, this is a simple matter, for you will either have chosen your *régime* before the wedding or will automatically fall under one of two *régimes légaux* (see CHAPTER 2). However, if you were married in the U.S. and did not come to live in France shortly thereafter, your *régime* will likely be that of the property laws that prevail in the place in which you lived for a year or more right after you were married: your *premier domicile conjugal*.

The following states have some form of community property laws: Arizona, California, Idaho, Louisiana, New Mexico, Nevada, Puerto Rico, Texas, Washington and Wisconsin. In these states, both real and personal property acquired before the marriage are treated as separate property of the acquiring spouse, which is the same principle as applies in a *communauté réduite aux acquêts*. In 1980, the state of New York passed a law introducing the concept of marital property (*acquêts*) being dually owned by both spouses. In Canada, the French-speaking province of Quebec uses a system called *société d'acquêts*, whereas the other provinces have a *régime des biens familiaux*. The division of community property acquired after marriage may be altered by antenuptial contracts.

All the other states have property laws comparable to the French *séparation des biens*, i.e. all assets, past and present, remain the personal property of their original owner, except for property acquired in joint names.

Making more than one will

Legally speaking, it is quite possible to have more than one will extant at a given time. As such a state of affairs presents technical drafting problems, an international wills and estate lawyer is indispensible for the drafting of additional wills. Typically, multiple wills are drawn up where the testator owns property in more than one country.

France has adopted the principle that real estate located in a sovereign state will be subject to the laws of that state. It therefore stands to reason that, if you possess real estate in the United States, you would be entitled to make a will in that country specifying how you wish it to be disposed of at your death. If there is a conflict with French inheritance laws, U.S. law (the laws that make it legal to will property to whomever one wishes) would prevail. By the same token, if a person domiciled outside France dies leaving real property in France, this property would be divided amongst his heirs according to French law, regardless of the inheritance laws of his home country.

However, it is not certain that property located outside France would be immune to forced heirship laws if its value surpassed the *quotité disponible*. It is possible that, in this case, one's children could take legal steps to have all or part of the property included in their inheritance. If you do possess real estate in the U.S., it would be advisable to consult an international lawyer before making an American will.

A preferable alternative for dealing with holdings in the U.S. is to set up a trust whose provisions are not in conflict with French inheritance laws. While this measure cannot change the way in which your estate is distributed, it has the advantage of helping you manage your assets during your lifetime and will avoid having them frozen while the estate is being settled. French law will recognize and apply trusts on the condition that their provisions do not violate forced heirship rules. These provisions can therefore apply to the *quotité disponible;* all of the trust's provisions can even be implemented if all of the *héritiers réservataires* agree in writing (assuming that they are all of age).

The attitude of French law towards this Anglo-American institution is in the process of evolving; France may soon ratify the Hague Convention of July 1, 1985, which applies to the recognition of trusts by civil law countries.

Anyone with significant holdings in both countries would be well advised to consult an international lawyer before making an appointment with a French *notaire* in order to be aware of all the possibilities available.

CHAPTER 5

Survivors' Benefits

There are several government-funded plans for providing aid to the recently widowed: The *Capital Décès* (Death Allocation), the *Allocation Veuvage* (Widow's Pension), the *Allocation de Décès* (Death Allowance), and the *Pension de Réversion* (Survivor's Retirement Pension). However, the private means of the surviving spouse must be quite modest to enable her to qualify. We will therefore not discuss these benefits in detail here, but refer you to Appendix 4 for more information.

CHAPTER 6

Providing for Orphaned Children

Parents of underage children are naturally concerned about what would happen in the extremely unlikely event that both the mother and father should die. In France, it is entirely possible to make a will for the sole express purpose of designating the person you would wish to have the care of your children should they be orphaned. In the absence of a will, it is the family court judge (*le juge de tutelle*) who decides who will be their guardian.

Assuming that you wish to make a holographic will (see CHAPTER 2), the appropriate wording could be as follows:

Je soussigné _____, demeurant à _____,
demande à ce que la tutelle de mes enfants, _____, en cas de décès
de moi-meme et de mon épouse, soit confiée à _____, demeurant à
_____, à qui je transmets tous les pouvoirs que me confert la loi.
J'entends que cette tutelle soit obligatoirement entérinée par le conseil de famille en cas
d'acceptation par (name of the designated guardian) de sa mission.

Translation: I, the undersigned _____
domiciled_____, request that the guardianship of my children
_____,in the event of the death of my spouse and
myself, be given to _____, domiciled
_____, to whom I transmit all legal powers of
tutelage.
I understand that this request will be automatically approved by the family council upon the acceptance of this tutelage by (name of designated guardian).

Remember that each parent must make a separate will and that the procedures described in the chapter on Wills must be scrupulously respected in order for it to be valid.

CHAPTER 7

Your Earthly Remains

The Living Will

In certain American states, it is possible to make a special kind of will, called a Directive to Physicians, which stipulates that you do not wish your life to be artificially prolonged should you be in a near-death state such as a coma. The purpose of such a document, obviously, is to state clearly your wishes in this respect while you are able, and to provide a legal cover for the doctors who are caring for you so that they will not hesitate to terminate life if they are sure that you have no chance of recovery.

In France, however, this does not appear to be an issue. According to a source at the *Ordre des Médecins*, the doctor in charge decides whether or not it is advisable to sustain a patient's life by artificial means. Whatever his decision, he is doubtless in much less danger here of having legal action taken against him, and therefore has more latitude to take whatever measures he feels are justified by humanitarian considerations and plain common sense.

This renders the making of a Living Will in France rather useless, as it would probably have no legal value, nor would it seem to be really necessary. On the other hand, there is certainly no harm in making one if you so wish.

It's Your Body

If you wish to will your cadaver to science, you should write to the Faculté de Médecine, Service du Don des Corps, 45, rue des Saint Pères, 75006 Paris, who will send you the appropriate forms to be filled out and returned to them.

....But Your Organs Belong to Everyone

Should you die accidently, French law allows the physician in charge to remove whatever organs he wishes for transplantation. In order to do this, he needs neither your consent nor that of your family (although they can object on religious or other grounds).

The only way to ensure that this will not happen -- should you be violently opposed -- is to have a written statement, preferably on your person at the time of death, stating your absolute refusal.

In other words, it is entirely unnecessary to make a will stipulating that you wish to donate your organs, as it may well be done automatically.

For more details on dealing with death, we refer you to Health Care Resources in Paris, published by WICE, 20, boulevard du Montparnasse, 75015 Paris; Tel: 45.66.75.50.

CHAPTER 8

Expenses Involved in Settling an Estate

French Inheritance Taxes and Other Costs

Inheritance Taxes

The French inheritance tax system allows for a pre-tax deduction from the amount which is due to each heir; as of this writing, the surviving spouse, children, grandchildren and parents may inherit up to 330,000 FF (more if they are handicapped) tax-free; all others may inherit up to 10,000 FF (with the exception of brothers and sisters, who may take a larger exemption if they fulfill certain conditions).

The following table shows the rates that apply to the taxable estate (calculated separately for each heir):

Descendants and ascendants (pre-tax deduction is 300,000FF)

Where the total taxable estate is:

Less than 50,000FF	5%
50,000 FF to 75,000 FF	10%
75,000 FF to 100,000 FF	15%
100,000 FF to 3,400,000FF	20%
3,400,000 FF to 5,600,000 FF	30%
5,600,000 FF to 11,200,000 FF	35%
More than 11,200,000 FF	40%

Any heir who is a direct ascendant or descendant and has three or more children may deduct 4,000 FF per child, starting with the third child, from the amount due on his share of the estate; for other heirs, the amount is 2,000 FF for the third and each subsequent child.

Between spouses (pre-tax deduction is 330,000FF)

Where the total taxable estate is:

Less than 50,000 FF	5%
50,000 FFto 100,000 FF	10%
100,000 FF to 200,000 FF	15%
200,000 FF to 3,400,000 FF	20%
3,400,000 FF to 5,600,000 FF	30%
5,600,000 FF to 11,200,000 FF	40%

Between brothers and sisters

Where the total taxable estate is:

Less than 150,000 FF	35%
More than 150,000 FF	45%

Between relatives to the fourth degree

Flat rate: 55%

All others: 60%

Lifetime gifts (*donations*) are subject to essentially the same laws and tax rates as apply to an inheritance.

<u>Filing Deadline</u>

The amount due on the estate must be calculated and paid to the tax authorities within six months after the date of death in order to avoid paying a fine.

Other Costs

There are other expenses besides inheritance taxes to be taken into account when calculating the total cost of settling an estate. Some of these -- such as the *acte de notoriété* (see glossary) are fixed, while others are based on the value of the estate. These could include: l'*attestation de propriété* (certification of ownership) for real estate; *notaire*'s fees for handling the will or lifetime bequest, filing the tax return, dividing the estate, etc. 18.6% V.A.T. must be added to all of these costs.

<u>U.S. Inheritance Taxes</u>

At death, a U.S. citizen domiciled in France will be subject to the above tax laws.*
However, certain categories of property can be exempted from French estate or gift tax:
(1) Real estate located in the U.S. (see Chapter 4)
(2) A U.S.-based business that did not have a permanent office in France.
(3) Certain types of tangible personal property (e.g., silverware, artworks) physically located in the U.S.

*<u>With the following exceptions:</u>

If you are a non-French citizen domiciled in France BUT:

- Are a diplomat.
- Had clearly intended to retain your domicile in the U.S. and were domiciled in France no more than 5 years out of the 7 preceding your death.
- Were in France on an employment assignment, and were domiciled in France no more than 5 years out of the 7 preceding your death. This exception applies also to the working person's spouse and/or dependent.
- If you were in France on a renewal of an assignment and were domiciled in

France less than 7 years out of the 10 years preceding your death.

Even if you and your spouse are living in the U.S. and therefore your fiscal domicile is there, you should be aware that your non-American spouse does not benefit from the marital deduction rules of U.S. law, under which property left to an American spouse is free of estate tax. In fact, the surviving spouse who is an alien may be liable for an immediate federal estate tax of up to 55% on all of the deceased's property exceeding a net value of $600,000 (although the top rate will drop to 50% in 1993).

There are steps that can be taken to partially circumvent this law -- in particular, providing for a Qualifying Domestic Trust. If you fall into this category and anticipate a net worth of over $600,000 at the time of your death, you should seek professional advice on this subject. (Don't forget that, in the U.S., life insurance proceeds must be included in the total, unless a life insurance trust has been set up to exclude the insurance from the estate of both spouses.)

CHAPTER 9

Things to Do

BEFORE the death of a spouse, i.e. **NOW**

1. If you are not yet married, consider very carefully the various options for choosing a marriage contract. Even if, at the present time, you have no significant holdings, the *régime* you choose will affect all property acquired during the marriage.

Ask a professional about such possibilities as *la communauté universelle avec faculté d'attribution au conjointe survivante* and *la communauté avec clause de préciput*. Keep in mind that once you are married, these options are much less viable.

2. If you are married, arrange for a *donation entre époux* or make wills in each other's favor if you have not done so already. In fact, if you or your spouse is not French, it is wise to back up a *donation* with a will.

3. Find out what life insurance coverage has been provided for by your spouse. Consider changing the policy or increasing its value if it seems necessary.

4. If all of your children are of age, consider having them waive their rights to their share of the inheritance until both you and your spouse have died. This will allow you to go into a *communauté universelle avec clause d'attribution intégrale en cas de décès*, in which case all of the deceased spouse's property goes to the surviving spouse who does not have to pay any inheritance taxes.

5. If you own real estate in the U.S. and do not wish it to be distributed according to French law, consider making a separate will to provide for its transfer.

6. If you were married in North America, find out what property laws apply to your marriage contract. If there is a conflict with the French *régime légal* which may have been assigned to you, get it straightened out through your *notaire*.

7. Keep in mind that any money contained in a bank account belonging to the deceased alone will be frozen until the estate is settled. A joint account, however, allows the surviving spouse free access to half of the balance (which is considered to be her property anyway), and in any case the account will not be frozen.

AFTER

For better or for worse, the amount of red tape to be dealt with immediately following the death of one's spouse leaves little time for wallowing in grief.

1. **Certification of death:** First, death must be certified by a doctor, who fills out a death certificate (*certificat médical de constatation du décès*). The date of death is important in that it serves as a reference for determining the beginning of the settling of the estate, the value of its contents, and the inheritance and tax laws that apply.

2. **Declaration of death:** Once you have the death certificate, you have twenty-four hours to get it to the local town hall. (Of course it will still be accepted if you are a little late.) If the deceased passed away in the hospital, the hospital staff usually takes care of this formality.

The person who makes the *déclaration du décès* must produce identification both for himself and the deceased. The town records clerk will issue a burial permit (*permis d'inhumer*) and a death certificate (*acte de décès*) which must be signed by the person making the declaration. This death certificate is the document that will allow the settlement of the deceased's estate to proceed.

The town registrar will send a copy of the death certificate to the town hall of the deceased's birthplace so that it can be filed with his birth certificate.

If the deceased was American, a form called Report of Death of an American Citizen Abroad should be obtained from the Consulate. This is very useful in certifying the death of U.S. citizens.

3. **Putting seals on the deceased's property**: If this is done at all, it should be done right away in order to have the desired effect, i.e. avoiding the misappropriation or tampering with goods or papers by persons having access to the deceased's home.

Strips of paper or cloth are affixed to the entrances of the dwelling or to desk drawers and cupboard doors, and sealed with wax. A simple inventory of the dwelling's contents may suffice. In certain extreme cases it is even possible to appoint a custodian to guard the premises.

Anyone - heir, spouse, creditor or executor - who has an interest in the estate can request that the property be sealed. Application should be made to the chief clerk of the *tribunal d'instance* of the district where the deceased lived.

4. **Going to see the *notaire*:** If the deceased's estate contained no real estate or other goods of any significant value, it is not necessary to call upon a *notaire* to oversee its settlement. In such case, the mayor or court clerk issues a *certificat d'hérédité* which will allow the distribution of whatever sums are involved.

The *notaire* to be contacted first would logically be that of the deceased, as he is most likely to have a copy of the deceased's will if there is one. However, an heir is free to call upon a *notaire* or attorney of his choice, who will represent his interests in case of conflict with the other heirs. Even in the absence of any conflict, anyone who does not feel entirely comfortable at the idea of dealing directly with a French *notaire* would be well advised to call upon a Paris-based U.S. estates attorney to interface. He can explain the whole procedure to the family, spot sensitive areas such as undeclared revenue and potential problems with children, and counsel the family as to how to present these issues to the *notaire*. There are problems that the *notaire* is not ready, able or willing to handle. Also, it is often best for the team of U.S. lawyer and *notaire* to work over the various issues that arise in the administration of an international estate and for the U.S. lawyer to act as liaison with the family, especially with members located in the U.S.

During the first meeting with the *notaire* post mortem, you will be asked to produce several documents which are essential to the steps which must be taken in the settlement of the estate: the issuance of an *acte de notoriété* (see glossary) designating the heirs to the estate; the preparation of an inventory of the estate's contents; the reading out of the will, if any; and the review of the various options open to the heirs and the surviving spouse.

The more information you are able to provide at the outset, the sooner the often lengthy process of settlement can begin. Among the records you will need:

- The *Acte de Décès* (see No. 2 above).
- Any records pertaining to a previous marriage: the divorce decree, etc.
- The deceased's birth certificate on which his death has been recorded (see No. 2 above).
- The heirs' and legatees' *Livret de Famille* and all other available documents pertaining to their civil status.
- The deceased's marriage contract.
- The emancipation certificate (see glossary) for any minor children involved.
- Any document expressing the deceased's wishes on the disposition of his estate: *Acte de donation*, last will and testament, etc.
- If the deceased was married under a community property regime: copies of any goods inherited or deeded to the spouses during the marriage; copies of *Actes de remploi*; a list of any work done on individually-owned property; an accounting of goods bought by the surviving spouse with his/her funds.
- The deceased's bank references and most recent bank statements; savings account passbook(s); names and addresses of securities brokers; life insurance policy.
- License and registration for vehicles and boats.
- Deeds to properties; copies of leases.
- All documents (insurance policies in particular) pertaining to the deceased's valuable possessions: furniture, jewels, art objects, race horses, etc.

The *notaire* will write to the various institutions (banks, insurance companies, etc.) to ascertain whether any real property is mortgaged and will have all other property assessed.

Having located the deceased's will, the *notaire* draws up an official report enumerating its contents and describing the circumstances of its filing by the deceased and its opening by the *notaire* himself. He then proceeds to register the will within three months from the date of death.

The will and report are kept on file by the *notaire* who sends a copy of the will to the clerk of the court of the deceased's place of residence.

After giving a reading of the will, the *notaire* informs each heir and legatee as to what their options are and the steps each must take before being allowed to take possession of his share of the inheritance.

These options are essentially three-fold:

1. **Simple acceptance of the inheritance**: This solution does not require any formalities but should not be adopted unless one is very familiar with the deceased's patrimony. The consenting heirs are responsible for all outstanding debts, even if they exceed the estate's assets, in which case the heir(s) would be required to settle them out of his (their) own pocket(s).

2. **Acceptance of the inheritance pending inventory**: Although this option requires that a declaration be filed with the court and that an inventory be formally requested, it is advisable when there is a doubt as to the solvency of the patrimony and compulsory when minors are involved.

The inventory must take place within three months of the death date and should be conducted in the presence of all those who stand to inherit. The potential heirs then have forty days in which to decide whether or not to accept their respective shares. Everything is frozen during this period-- no one receives any part of the estate, and any creditors must wait.

3. **Refusal**: This usually happens when it is obvious that one will be coming into more liabilities than assets. In this case, one receives nothing, but neither does one owe anything, not even inheritance taxes.

If they have decided to accept the inheritance, the *héritiers réservataires* will have what is known as *la saisine de la succession*, or immediate title to all the rights and privileges of ownership of the inherited property. If there is more than one heir, they will be equal-part owners of the whole of their collective inheritance, rather than full owners of an individual portion. This state of affairs, called an *indivision* (see glossary), will continue until the final apportioning has been accomplished by the *notaire*, enabling the heirs to *sortir de l'indivision*.

Those heirs or *légataires* who are not *réservataires* but who have been included in the will do not have *saisine*. They must furnish proof -- usually a certificate issued by the *notaire* -- that they are entitled to their share.

If the surviving spouse is designated the *légataire universel* (see glossary) in a holographic or a secret will, she will need to call upon the services of an attorney and file a claim with the competent judge. It is therefore preferable for the deceased to have made a *testament authentique* or a *donation entre époux*.

If the couple had made a *donation entre époux* or if the deceased's will provided for a *quotité disponible spéciale* (see chart, p. 174) settled on the surviving spouse, and if there are children, the spouse must choose among three possibilities: a life interest in the entire estate; a life interest in 3/4 of the estate and full ownership of 1/4; or full ownership of 1/2, 1/3, or 1/4 of the estate, the proportions depending on the number of children. Each case being different, it is best to review these options with the *notaire* who will explain various personal and fiscal consequences.

It is possible for the testator to have stipulated within the will or *donation* which solution should be selected, in which case the problem of choice would not arise.

CHAPTER 10

MEMBERS' TESTIMONY

Several AAWE members who have been widowed have kindly agreed to pass on some of their experiences in dealing with French inheritance laws to the readers of this guide. We are grateful to them for sharing with us some of the knowledge that they have gained as a result of this very painful loss.

ROBERTA BEARDSLEY is an interesting case in that her late husband was American -- as is she -- but, as the couple had been legally domiciled in France for several years, Jim's estate came under French law. Roberta writes:

I guess the first thing to do is to talk about the subject before anyone falls ill. Going to see the *notaire* when someone's life is compromised is an extremely painful experience. In addition, if certain changes are to be made, it may take from six months to a year to get everything in order.

In our case, we were married in California. After my husband's death, it was determined in a *certificat de coutume* drawn up by a California bar member practicing in Paris that our *régime du marriage* was equivalent to that which exists in France when a couple marries without any contract, i.e. *la communauté réduite aux acquêts*. This *certificat de coutume* is a mandatory first step in settling an estate or in changing one's *régime*. However, the consequences of this determination were not the same in France as they would have been in California, for under California law the surviving spouse would have inherited the 50% belonging to the deceased spouse. In France, that 50% passes to the children.

My husband and I had done a *donation*, which gave me the *quotité disponible*. The most important outcome of this action was that I had the freedom to choose how the 50% would be used. In my case, I kept the *usufruit* and a part of the *nue-propriéte*; the children became *nue-propriétaires* of the portion reserved to them by law.

My children and I are now bound by an unholy alliance known as *indivision* because of my decision not to give them full title to their share of their father's estate. Every time I sell something, even a *résidence principale* if they no longer live at home, I am obliged to calculate their taxes separately and, out of fairness, pay them myself since one can hardly expect the children to pay for something which brought them no benefit.

These complications and a healthy estate tax could have been avoided if we had completed formalities for changing our *régime* before my husband's death. If we had opted for the *communauté universelle*, I would have inherited everything directly with no taxes to pay. Given my age at the time of my husband's death (relatively young) and the size of the estate (modest), this solution would have made the most sense. If I were further along the slippery slope and the estate were larger, it would have made sense from a tax-planning standpoint to have the children inherit directly from their father since there are deductions for each person who inherits.

If you are under the *régime* of *communauté réduite aux acquêts*, there is a way of giving everything to the spouse: *attribution de communauté*; but this involves court approval and the payment of *droits de succession*.

Of course, some of these decisions are made at the gut level. The French seem to be obsessed with protecting the children to the detriment of the spouse, while the American system seems to adopt a cavalier attitude to children's interests. How many "Leisure World" marriages have we heard of where an entire estate escapes the rightful heirs? My husband was American too, so we didn't have to deal with cultural differences about how and when the children should inherit. The children as *majeurs* were ready to give up their rights, as is required in establishing a *communauté universelle*. There was just too much pain and not enough time to see it through.

Unlike Roberta, whose husband passed away after a long illness, **LAURA DONDEY** lost her husband suddenly. Her advice:

Above all, make no vital decisions in the first year. Financial and other conditions may not be as bleak as they seem.

Other practical considerations:
- A better-than-decent life insurance policy.
- Joint ownership of bank accounts and car.
- Be familiar with all aspects of family business and/or insurance policies, retirement benefits to come etc. Of course, I was NOT.
- Have a will with spouse, of course.

Pray God for good capable friends to stand in while you are in a state of shock.

SANDRA CAILLENS FRELAND'S children were only three and five when her husband was killed in an accident several years ago. Fortunately, he had very good comprehensive life insurance coverage (which, she points out, is often not the case in France, where death is generally considered a family matter, and it is assumed that care, both financial and emotional, will be provided by either parents or in-laws). She was nevertheless shocked to realize to what degree the surviving spouse can be disadvantaged by the existing beliefs, customs, and/or laws.

She mentioned, for instance, that she had been expected to, and did, repay a loan which had been made to her husband *en avance d'hoirie* by her father-in-law (who had remarried); i.e. whatever remained unpaid at the time of the latter's death would be considered part of her husband's share of his father's estate.

Like Laura, she advises readers NOT to make any major decisions following a spouse's death, e.g. changing residence, neighborhood, job, children's schools and other regular activities, in particular the tempting one of getting away from it all by moving back to the U.S. If possible, it is better to wait a good two years before making any major changes in one's life style. What can be beneficial in the interim are simpler, if affordable, changes: a new car, for example, or a new wardrobe.

She suggests taking out a separate, smaller insurance policy to cover immediate costs and inheritance taxes.

VIRGINIA VITTOZ was good enough to write the following testimony in the midst of dealing with the interminable administrative details which fell to her upon her recent widowhood:

My advice is about advice itself ....the kind a widow receives.

There are two special bits of counsel that come up constantly. The first, well known and quite banal, is nevertheless very important. "Keep busy" has been said a million times and still remains the very best advice.

The second bit of advice a widow is likely to hear comes over and over from persons cautioning her about rapid decisions. Wait, they say. Don't make any major decisions or change your life style in any way for at least a year ... or better two years.

I have certain reservations about this attitude. Upon closer examination, one finds this credo comes essentially from the U.S. where many widows, it seems, are prone to hasty decisions...which they later regret. A woman, for instance, may sell off her New England home and rush out to live in California. Or she may get rid of the comfortable family furniture and change her décor to maxi-modern. Or she might take the bank account and go on a round-the-world tour with an eye out for a new husband.

In France the situation is different. The take-it-easy advice is less important for the simple reason that a new widow is far more likely to discover constraints than to find herself wallowing in an excess of heady freedom. If she wants to sell the house and flee, she may find that the house doesn't really belong to her. The same is true for the furniture. There are the children to be reckoned with. In addition, the money needed to finance hasty ventures will often not be available to her. Even the get-away car may not be entirely hers.

In the U.S. women usually inherit directly from their husbands. Children may receive gifts or a part of their inheritance, but in the majority of cases, the bulk of the estate goes to the wife. Also, in America, one doesn't hear the word *usufruit* echoing at every turn. It's a word I personally have learned to loathe. No matter how desirable it may be for some persons or how beneficial, it still is, in my opinion, a form of bondage. If you want to stay put --or if the status quo suits you--so much the better. But if you choose to sell, to move, or to direct your destiny in some other direction, you may find, if you have children, that your husband's will or *donation* becomes so watered down that it is virtually no longer valid and doesn't give you much financial security. The law takes over and France's children...even if they are 40, 50 or 60 years old (and enjoy a life style far superior to that of their parents,) must still be awarded their due...often to the detriment of the mother.

In France, a succession must be signed, sealed, decided and paid within **six months** after a death. This means that important decisions must be made within that short period of time and I feel it is wrong to encourage a widow to dawdle when she should be giving lots of thought to her future. Every decision need not be immediately implemented, but the broad lines should be carefully considered...while the options are still open.

If I were to offer any other advice, it would be to keep track of all bills, notices, official letters, etc. There's no telling when they may be needed.

* *

We are also fortunate to have the testimony of a woman who is neither an AAWE member nor a widow, but who is American and lives in France with her Swiss husband. Their two adult children are currently attending college in the U.S.

Although neither elderly nor childless, this couple recently succeeded in changing their *régime* from *communauté réduite aux acquêts* to *communauté universelle avec attribution au survivant*, thus ensuring that the surviving spouse will come into possession of all of the couple's property and will not have to deal with the problems of being in *indivision* with the children, who will inherit upon the death of the second parent.

The whole process took about a year and two months and cost approximately 15,500 FF. It was feasible only because two essential conditions were met: (1) the children involved were of age, and (2) they were willing to waive their rights to the status of *héritier réservataire*. The procedure the woman describes is as follows:

1.   Consultation with a lawyer, preferably practicing in an international law firm, who will point out the advantages and disadvantages of making this change and will guide you in the steps to be taken prior to seeing the *notaire*.

2.   Visit to the *notaire*'s office armed with a *Lettre de Consentement des Enfants*, which can be worded as follows:

Je soussigné, _____
né le _____ à _____
de: Monsieur _____
et de: Madame _____
demeurant principalement et actuellement: _____
déclare être parfaitement informé de la volonté commune de mes parents d'adopter le régime de la Communauté universelle de biens présents et à venir.

Je suis également informé des consequences d'un tel changement de régime; notamment, il implique la réunion indivisible et universelle de tous les biens et conduit, en cas de décès de l'un de mes parents, à attribuer ceux-ci au survivant.

Je déclare par la présente ne m'opposer en aucune façon à ce changement de régime matrimonial.

> *Fait à _____*
> *Le _____*

The *notaire* then submits the application to the *Tribunal de Grande Instance*. If this court rules favorably, the change is registered with the couple's marriage certificate after a waiting period of three months and will be published according to law.

The culmination of this lengthy procedure is the issuance of an *Acte d'Attribution de Communauté*.

Appendix I

French Forced Heirship Laws

The following rules apply to the property of a person who has died intestate (leaving no will). As in many other areas, French legislation leaves nothing to chance, having set forth a set of extremely precise rules to govern a *succession ab intestat*.

These rules provide that:
- A significant portion of the inheritance goes to those who are related to the deceased by blood, leaving the spouse (who is considered an outsider) in a less favorable position. **(See the framed text in CHAPTER I, for recent developments in this area)**.
- Those who are favored by the law are arranged in a distinct hierarchy, as follows:
  1. **Descendants:** children, grandchildren, and great-grandchildren.
  2. **Privileged ancestors and collaterals:** parents and siblings.
  3. **Ordinary ancestors:** grandparents and great-grandparents.
  4. **Other relatives:** uncles, aunts, cousins, nieces, nephews.

If the deceased leaves just one heir in the first group, his/her claim takes priority over that of the members of all subsequent groups who are entitled to nothing, and so on down the line. Thus, the deceased's children always take precedence over father, mother and siblings, who themselves come before grandparents, who in turn override uncles, aunts and cousins.

If Mr. Dupont dies leaving one son, both parents, several brothers and sisters as well as various other relatives, only the son stands to inherit the share which is reserved for blood relatives; if, however, Mr. Dupont leaves no children or grandchildren, only his parents and siblings (who fall into Group 2) will inherit the share which is reserved for blood relatives, with nothing going to survivors who belong to Groups 3 and 4.

It should be stated here that if the deceased leaves a spouse, she will have some claim to part of the estate, an amount which will vary according to the status of the other heirs with whom she is competing. Before looking at the spouse's rights, let's examine those of the other family members.

First Group: Descendants

First in line are the children who share equally in the portion of the inheritance which is reserved for blood relatives (*la réserve*). If all of the deceased's children are living, grandchildren (or anyone else, for that matter) do not inherit any of *la réserve*.

However, if one of the deceased's children has died, leaving children of his own (the deceased's grandchildren), these heirs take over the rights of their late parent and share equally in the portion which normally would have gone to him. This is known as the principle of *la représentation* and applies ad infinitum.

If, of Mr. Lemercier's three children, one has predeceased him, leaving two children of his own (Mr. Lemercier's grandchildren), they will each get half of the share which normally would have gone to their late father. (Their mother, Mr. Lemercier's daughter-in-law, is completely bypassed in this case.)

If, however, one of Mr. Lemercier's grandchildren died before him, the late grandchild's children, if any, will get his share, and so on .....

- Illegitimate, adopted and adulterine children

The above categories of descendants do not have precisely the same claim on their parents' estate as fully legitimate children. The law makes distinctions among these various types of descendants and dictates what is their share in the inheritance.
(See framed text in CHAPTER 1).

Second Group: Privileged ancestors and collaterals

If the deceased leaves no descendants, neither children or grandchildren, his property will go to relatives who are classified as being in the second group, i.e. the deceased's father and mother (*ascendants privilégiés*) and siblings (*collatéraux privilégiés*).

Here again the principle of *représentation* applies, and the children of a deceased sibling will receive the portion which normally would have gone to their parent.

The *réserve* is divided as follows: half for the parents, half for the siblings.

Third Group: Ordinary ancestors (grandparents, great-grandparents, etc.)

If the deceased leaves no survivors in either the first or second group, *la réserve* will go to other ancestors and will be portioned out according to the principle of the *fente successorale* (division of inheritance): half goes to the mother's side, half to the father's; the closest relative on each side inherits all of the share to which his side is entitled.

Fourth Group: All other relatives

In the absence of either descendants, ancestors, privileged collaterals or of a spouse (who takes precedence over members of the fourth group), the estate will be divided amongst the other relatives of the deceased: uncles, aunts, great-uncles; great aunts, cousins, second cousins, etc. Here again, the patrimony is divided equally between the maternal and the paternal sides, with the closest relative on each side inheriting the entirety of that side's share.

Appendix 2

Rules governing life interest (*usufruit*)

1.   The assessment of the value of a life interest is based on all existing property at the time of the deceased's death, having subtracted debts and bequests (which are not included in the estate), but adding the value of gifts deeded to other heirs. This is the principal on which the legal life interest of the surviving spouse is calculated.

2.   *L'usufruit* cannot undermine the rights of an unconditional heir (*héritier réservataire*, i.e. descendants or ancestors). For example, the law does not permit the conversion of the share of the deceased's father, who is always a *héritier réservataire*, into simple ownership (*nue-propriété*) so as to enable the spouse to benefit from her legal share of the life interest.

These two rules may result in the surviving spouse's already minor share being further reduced because the other heirs' share cannot be compromised. Again, remember that the law does not consider the surviving spouse to be an unconditional heir, permitting her to be disinherited. Thus, a wife whose husband has neglected to provide for her can find herself in serious financial difficulty when her spouse dies. If the couple's marriage contract is one of *communauté des biens* (see glossary), the surviving spouse is nevertheless entitled to an *indemnité de deuil* (bereavement allowance) as well as a nine-month grace period during which she can continue to live off the couple's resources. Afterwards, if her remaining funds are not adequate, she can request a maintenance pension. She has a year after her spouse's death to file this request and can still make application as long as the apportionment of the estate amongst all the heirs has not been finalized. This pension is borne by all of the heirs. Its amount is calculated according to the spouse's needs and the size of the estate. The judge who determines how much it should be can also provide for built-in cost of living increases.

Appendix 3

Deeds of Gift

What is a *donation*?

A *donation* is an act by which an individual (*le donateur*) divests himself of a sum of money, real estate, or other assets and gives it to another person (*le donataire*).

A *donation* made to a person other than one's spouse is virtually irrevocable* and must be certified in writing by a *notaire* (*l'acte authentique*); the *donation* must be formally accepted by the recipient, also in writing, in order to be valid.

 *Exceptions:
- If the donor had no children at the time the *donation* was formalized but does have some afterwards.
- If the beneficiary shows ingratitude: if he betrays, physically harms, or otherwise wrongs the donor.
- If conditions attached to the gift are not respected by the beneficiary. (It is illegal to include conditions which would tend to limit basic human rights, such as marrying or having children.)
- The donor can opt for the right for himself and/or his dependents to simply occupy the property throughout their lives.
- A third possibility would be to give the property in exchange for a life-annuity (*rente viagère*), the amount of which would be determined with the help of a *notaire*.
- It is also possible to give goods which are not yet fully paid. It would be up to the beneficiary to assume responsibility for paying the balance due. (Don't forget that one has the right to refuse such a gift!)
- Still another condition could be that, should the recipient die before the benefactor, the gift would automatically revert to the latter (*clause de retour conventionnel* or *condition suspensive de survie du bénéficiaire*).
- It is even possible to stipulate that a gift to one's children or siblings be passed on to their own children (the donor's grandchildren or nephews and nieces). This is called *la substitution fidei-commissaire*.

To authenticate the gift, the *notaire* draws up an original document called a *minute*, which he keeps in his office; the parties concerned will receive certified copies, called *expéditions*.

Various types of *donation*

It is actually legal to simply make a hand-to-hand gift (*don manuel*) to whomever one wishes, without going through the legal formalities described above. Contrary to a *donation*, no taxes are payable at the time of transfer of ownership; however, if the recipient is an heir, he will have to pay inheritance taxes upon the death of his benefactor.

This way of transferring ownership may cause problems when the estate is being settled if the *héritiers réservataires* feel that their rightful share has been compromised. If the benefactor anticipates difficulties of this nature, he can request a receipt from the beneficiary.

It is also possible to give property conditionally -- with certain well-defined strings attached:

- The donor can retain life-interest in the property (*donation avec réserve d'usufruit*), and thus have the right to occupy or rent it and collect the payments. He/she can even stipulate that this prerogative be extended to her spouse, which, in the case of their home, means that the surviving spouse can continue to live there for the rest of his/her life.

If the gift is made *en avance d'hoirie*, this means that it simply constitutes an advance on what the beneficiary would eventually receive from the donor's estate. In other words, it will be deducted from the beneficiary's share of the estate after the owner's death.

However, it is possible to favor an heir by giving him a *donation par préciput et hors part*. This gift will not be deducted from his/her share of the estate but will be considered part of the remainder (*la quotité disponible*). (This is also the only way to make a gift to anyone who is not an heir.) Nevertheless, if this gift exceeds the amount of the remainder, the excess will revert to the portion which is reserved for the privileged heirs and be deducted from the *réserve* of the beneficiary, if he is himself a privileged heir.

La Donation-partage

La Donation-partage has become a very popular way for French parents to ensure, while still living, that their children receive an appropriate portion of their estate and at the same time benefit from certain fiscal advantages.

Only currently existing property can be transferred in this way: the *donation partage* does not apply to assets which may be acquired in the future. As the transfer is immediate, the parents often choose to retain a lifetime use (*usufruit*) of the property, or, alternatively, they can stipulate that a life annuity be paid on it. If they do opt for the life interest, a deduction is allowed on the value of the property subject to tax.

The gift can be made either jointly by both parents, or separately by each. It can include all or only part of their goods.

While each *héritier réservataire* must receive his due portion, it is possible to favor one of them (a handicapped child, for example) out of the *quotité disponible*.

A *donation-partage* allows for a reduction in inheritance taxes according to whatever fiscal laws apply at the time the gift is made, and depending on the age of the donor. Whatever taxes there are can be paid by the parents without this being considered part of the gift (and therefore taxable). This solution is obviously more advantageous to the children than having to pay inheritance taxes on an estate. If the parents have chosen to conserve life interest in the assets which they have thus transferred, they will benefit from the combined fiscal advantages which apply to both the *donation à réserve d'usufruit* and the *donation partage*.

One estate planning hint is to gift appreciating property -- such as securities -- so that future appreciation will accrue to the donees, and will thus not be taxed to the estate of the donor-parent.

Any lifetime gift by an American citizen has potential U.S. gift tax consequences. A U.S. tax specialist should be consulted in conjunction with any such transfer.

N.B.* It is important to include a clause in the *Acte de Donation* which forbids the beneficiary (the *nue-propriétaire*) from selling or mortgaging the property without the consent of the *usufruitier* (the donor), in order that the latter not be deprived of his life-interest against his wishes.

Appendix 4

Survivors' Benefits

Allocation de Veuvage (Widow's/Widower's Allowance)

This benefit is intended to provide assistance to those who had not yet reached retirement age when their spouse died, and consequently are not yet eligible for the *Pension de Réversion*. In order to qualify for the *Allocation de Veuvage*, therefore, one must be under the age of fifty-five. Other requirements are:

One's spouse must have been covered by the *Sécurité Sociale* (National Health System), either as a salaried employee or as a farm worker. Other categories of employees may also be eligible -- this information may be obtained from the *Caisse d'Assurance Vieillesse*.

One must have had the care of at least one child for nine years before his sixteenth birthday.

One must be a resident of France.

One's private income must not have exceeded 3,416 FF per month during the three months preceding the death or the date of application for the *Allocation*.

The Widow's Allowance is paid for a period of three years starting on the first day of the month of a spouse's death, if application was made during the following year; if application was made over a year after the date of death, it will start at the date of application. If the surviving spouse has reached the age of fifty at the time of death, he/she may receive payments up to the fifty-fifth birthday.

This benefit consists of monthly payments of 2,733 FF* for the first year, 1,796 FF* for the second year, and 1,367 FF* for the third year.

After the age of fifty-five, the surviving spouse is no longer eligible for the *Allocation de Veuvage*, but may be able to receive a *Pension de Réversion*.

Pension de Réversion

This benefit consists of what would have been the portion of the deceased's retirement pension which reverts to the surviving spouse. It usually amounts to about 52% of the deceased's pension, and is increased by 10% if the couple had at least three children.

To qualify for this benefit, one must:

- be fifty-five or over;
- not have remarried (but one can remarry after the pension has been attributed and still continue to receive it);
-have been married to the deceased for at least two years (less if there was a child);
- have a private income not exceeding 2,080 times the hourly SMIC (minimum wage), i.e. it must be less than 66,435 FF* per year.

However, one does not have to have been married to the deceased at the time of his death; if neither had remarried, the survivor would be eligible to receive this pension just as if they had not been divorced. If the deceased ex-spouse had remarried, the pension would be divided among his new partner and all preceding ones (providing they met the requirements); the amounts allotted to each would be directly proportional to the duration of each marriage.

Application should be made to the *Caisse d'Assurance Vieillesse* to which one's late spouse's last employer belonged.

Le Capital Décès

This is a lump sum paid to the next of kin (usually the spouse) of a deceased person who was insured under the *Séurité Sociale* system and who was under the age of sixty at the time of death.

This benefit may be claimed any time during the first two years following the date of death by making application to the deceased's *C.P.A.M.* (local Health Insurance office) which will provide the necessary forms.

The surviving spouse is considered to have priority over all other relatives for this benefit on condition that she was a dependent of the deceased and does not have private means in excess of 32,670 FF* per year. However, if the surviving spouse has not applied for this benefit within the first month following the date of death, other dependents may be entitled to claim it.

The amount of this benefit is equal to three months of the deceased's salary; it cannot be less than 1,361 FF* or more than 34,020 FF*. It is not considered part of the deceased's estate.

If there are no relatives close enough to claim the *Capital Décès*, the person who paid for the funeral expenses can be reimbursed by *Sécurité Sociale* if there were not sufficient funds in the deceased's estate to cover costs of even a modest funeral. The amount of this benefit will not exceed 5,400 FF* and must be approved by a special committee.

If the deceased was a recipient of a retirement pension, the amount he would have received for the month in which he died is paid to his estate, to be used to help offset expenses incurred.

Allocation de Décès

One may be eligible for this allowance if one's late spouse received unemployment compensation. The amount is proportional to the number of dependent children. Application should be made to the deceased's _A.S.S.E.D.I.C._ (unemployment compensation office).

*As of January 1, 1991.

GLOSSARY OF TERMS

abattement: exemption; portion of the estate which is not subject to tax. The amount one can inherit tax-free varies according to one's degree of kinship with the deceased. See tax table.

ab intestat: intestate, without a will.

actif successoral: all property owned by a person at the time of death.

acquêts: real estate and other goods acquired during a marriage. In a *régime de la communauté* marriage, these goods are jointly owned by the spouses.

acte authentique: a legal document drawn up by an official, usually a *notaire*, who authenticates its contents and date.

acte de notoriété: document issued by the *notaire* prior to the settlement of the estate; it establishes the deceased's identity and that of the heir(s) to an estate. Drawn up before two witnesses who must be French citizens and unrelated by blood or by marriage to each other nor to the deceased (usually friends or neighbors of the family), this document serves as proof to financial institutions, pension funds, insurance companies, etc., that one is in fact entitled to inherit.

adulterin: adjective used to describe an illegitimate child born of an adulterous relationship.

assurance veuvage: insurance paid by a retirement pension fund to widows and widowers who are under the age of fifty-five, and who fulfill certain conditions (see Appendix 4).

assurance vie: life insurance; voluntary insurance which, upon the death of the policyholder, entitles the beneficiary to a lump sum payment or a monthly stipend.

attestation de propriété: document drawn up by the *notaire* which certifies transfer of ownership of real property.

attribution préférentielle: rule which allows certain heirs to choose a specific item out of the estate on the condition that they reimburse the other heirs if necessary. Thus a spouse can elect to keep her home if she wishes.

avenant: modification to a contract.

bien propre: property which belongs to only one spouse and is therefore not included in the common holdings of the couple.

biens immobiliers: real estate.

biens mobiliers: all other property.

capital décès: sum paid by the national health fund (*Sécurité Sociale*), banks, and/or private insurance companies, at the death of the insured person. The beneficiary's eligibility for this insurance depends on the fulfillment of certain conditions. See Appendix 4.

codicille: partial modification of a will.

cohéritiers: all persons who stand to inherit from the same estate.

collatéraux: all relatives who are not direct ancestors or descendants: siblings, aunts and uncles, cousins.

collatéraux ordinaires: aunts, uncles and cousins.

communauté: community property system, in which certain goods are considered the joint property of the two spouses.

communauté légale: property rights that apply to couples who married with no contract.

communauté réduite aux acquêts: property rights that apply to couples married after 1965 with no contract. Under this *régime*, only goods acquired during the marriage are considered joint property of the spouses.

communauté universelle: system under which spouses share all their belongings, past and present.

déclaration de succession: document that must be submitted to the tax authorities within six months following death and which enumerates the assets and the liabilities contained in the estate. It is used to compute the amount of inheritance tax due.

Dévolution légale: the set of rules that applies to the estate of someone who died without having made a will or a lifetime bequest.

don manuel: hand-to-hand gift of goods or money made without the formality of a legal bequest.

donataire: the recipient of a *donation* (lifetime gift).

donateur: benefactor.

donation: notarized act by which the ownership of goods is irrevocably transmitted from one person to another.

donation au dernier vivant : a notarized document that allows spouses to give each other more extensive inheritance rights than they would normally enjoy. Basically, it allows the surviving spouse to benefit from the entirety of the couple's holdings while keeping the property intact for the children to inherit at the death of the second parent (i.e. the surviving spouse).

donation entre époux: a clause that can be included in a marriage contract and which provides for irrevocable lifetime gifts to one's spouse. It can apply to both present and future holdings.

donation avec réserve d'usufruit: lifetime gift which stipulates that the benefactor reserves the right to benefit from its use (in the case of a dwelling, to occupy or rent it) as long as he lives.

donation en avance d'hoirie: lifetime gift granted as an advance on future inheritance. When it is time for the estate to be settled, this gift is taken into account in computing each heir's share and would therefore be deducted from the beneficiary's portion of the estate.

donation par préciput et hors part: similar to the above, except that it is not considered an advance on a future inheritance. This fact must be stipulated in the deed of gift.

donation-partage: living gift which consists of deeding all or part of one's goods to one's children.

droits de donation: taxes levied on a gift.

droits de succession: inheritance taxes.

émancipé: adjective used to describe an underage individual who has been given certain adult rights by legal decree.

exonération: the partial or total exemption from inheritance taxes which applies to certain categories of property.

expédition: copy of a notarized document of which the original (*minute*) is kept in the *notaire*'s office.

fente successorale: see Appendix I.

fichier central des testaments: centralized registry for all wills which are filed with a *notaire* in France.

héritier: heir.

héritier réservataire: compulsory heir; one who, by virtue of his degree of kinship with the deceased, cannot be disinherited. For instance, an only child would necessarily be entitled to no less than one-half of his parents' estate.

hypothèque: mortgage

indivision: transitional state between the time of death and the settlement of an estate. During this period all the heirs (called *indivisaires* or *héritiers indivis*) are considered owners of the entire estate prior to its being divided amongst them.

indivision conventionnnelle: when all the heirs agree in writing to remain in a state of *indivision*.

inventaire: an exhaustive report drawn up by the *notaire* which itemizes all the assets and liabilities comprising an estate or the common property of a couple.

légataire: legatee; recipient of a legacy.

légataire à titre universel: heir who automatically inherits a specific portion (one-third, one-quarter, all the furniture, etc.) of an estate.

légataire particulier: heir who receives a specified item or sum of money.

légataire universel: residual legatee: he who inherits the entire *quotité disponible*.

legs: legacy.

legs à titre universel: legacy comprising only a portion of an estate.

legs particulier: legacy of a specified sum of money, object, or other item.

legs universel: legacy of the entire *quotité disponible*.

libéralité: bequest or legacy.

licitation: auctioning off of a piece of property belonging to all of the heirs together (*en indivision*).

masse successorale: the total of all assets, including money owed, which constitute an estate.

minute: original of a notarized document which is kept in the *notaire*'s office.

nantir: to secure, as a loan.

notaire: a public official appointed by the Ministry of Justice. Their functions include the preparation and recording of notarial acts (wills, deeds, acts of incorporation, marriage contracts, etc.), the administration and settling of estates, and serving as the repository of wills. Fees are fixed by law.

nu-propriétaire: person who is considered to have the ownership but not the use of a piece of property.

nue-propriété: ownership of a piece of property in which someone else has life interest.

partage: procedure which dissolves an *indivision* and divides the contents of an estate amongst the heirs.

partage amiable: the above procedure based on an amicable agreement reached by the heirs.

partage judiciare: apportionment by judgement, which occurs when the heirs do not agree on the manner in which an estate should be divided.

partage par homologation: division which must be approved by a judge, as when some of the heirs are minors.

passif: liabilities.

patrimoine: patrimony

pension de réversion: portion of the deceased's retirement pension which is paid to the surviving spouse.

pleine propriété: full ownership, i.e. both possession and use of an item of property.

préciput: a *donation* which is not considered an advance on a future inheritance; in the case of a *donation par préciput et hors part* between spouses, it would not be included in the pool of commonly-owned goods to be divided prior to settlement of the estate, but would go intact to the surviving spouse.

quotité disponible ordinaire: part of one's estate that can be willed to whomever one wishes.

quotité disponible spéciale: part of one's estate that becomes greater than the *quotité disponible* ordinaire if the testator chooses to will it to his/her spouse.

rapport: procedure followed during the settlement of an estate which takes into account bequests made as an advance on an inheritance.

rapport en nature: when the heir who has received a specific item as an advance on his inheritance returns that item to the estate.

rapport en valeur: the above heir keeps the specific item but owes its cash value to the estate.

régime matrimonial: property rules which govern a marriage, either as part of a contract or, in the absence of a contract, as prescribed by the law.

renoncer à la succession: to refuse an inheritance, thereby avoiding liability for the deceased's debts.

représentation: the faculty of children to inherit their deceased parent's share of an estate.

reprise: the restitution of individually-owned property to each spouse before commonly-owned property is divided.

reprise en deniers: when the *reprise* consists of a sum equivalent in value to the individually-owned property.

reprise en nature: when the individually-owned item itself is taken back by the spouse to whom it belongs.

réservataire: see héritier réservataire.

réserve: portion of an estate which by law must go to the *héritiers réservataires*.

réserve d'usufruit: a clause which enables the donor to give property away yet keep the use of it during his lifetime.

saisine: the right to claim ownership of property included in an estate without waiting for legal authorization.

scellés: seals of paper or cloth put on furniture or doors to prevent goods from being misappropriated.

séparation de biens: marriage contract that stipulates that each spouse's belongings remain individually-owned property.

soulte: sum of money paid in compensation for all or part of an inheritance.

testament, testament authentique, testament mystique, testament olographe : see CHAPTER 2.

testateur: testator, one who makes a will.

tontine: clause which stipulates that a home acquired as joint property by a couple will remain the property of the surviving spouse and will not be included in the estate of the deceased.

usufruit: the right to enjoy the use of a piece of property during one's lifetime without actually owning it.

viager: contract which allows one to sell one's dwelling, yet continue to occupy it (or not) while receiving as payment a regular income for the rest of one's life.

USEFUL ADDRESSES

Journal Officiel   Tel:40.58.76.00 or 40.58.75.00 or 45.75.62.31.
26 rue Desaix, 75015 Paris
--Good documentation service for those who wish written copies of specific laws.

Centre d'Information du Notariat Parisien
1, boulevard de Sébastopol, 75001 Paris
--Free consultations with *notaires*, if you have the patience to wait.

La Clinique du Droit Tel:45.00.64.32.
59, avenue Victor Hugo, 75016 Paris
--Permanent source of legal and practical information accessible by mail, telephone or by
appointment.

Le Centre Interministériel de Renseignements Administratifs (C.I.R.A.)
Tel:43.46.13.46.
--Tax Information by telephone.

Caisse Nationale de l'Assurance Maladie des Travailleurs Salariés (C.N.A.M.T.S.)
Tel: 43.21.01.10. / 43.20.11.33.
66 avenue du Maine, 75682 Paris Cedex 14

Centre d'Information et de Renseignements de la Caisse Primaire
d'Assurance Maladie (C.P.A.M.)   Tel: 42.80.63.67.
69 bis, rue de Dunkerque, 75453 Paris Cedex 09

Fédération des Associations de Veuves Chefs de Famille (F.A.V.E.C.)
Tel: 45.26.05.42.
28, place Saint Georges, 75009 Paris

Caisse Nationale d'Assurance Vieillesse des Travailleurs Salariés
(C.N.A.V.T.S.)
Tel: 40.37.37.37.
110-112 rue de Flandre, 75951 Paris Cedex 19

BIBLIOGRAPHY

BISSELL, Thomas. "Tax Laws and the Alien Spouse," International Herald Tribune, November 17-18, 1990.

"Couples pour Bien Vivre Vos Droits", 50 Millions de Consommateurs, Hors Série No. 60, février 1993.

GUERIN, Jean-Michel and NERESSIS, Catherine. *L'Héritage.* *21ème édition, Collection des Guides Pratiques du Logement, ed. De Particulier à Particulier*, 1988.

"Héritage et Succession", 50 Millions de Consommateurs, Hors Série No. 54, décembre 1991.

Histoire du Droit Privé. Collection Que Sais-je?

HOLLAND, Philip. Living in France, 5th edition. London: Robert Hale, 1990.

REVILLARD, Maris. *Droit International Privé et Pratique Notariale.*

Succession et Héritage. Série Guides Pratiques de Notre Temps, ed. Bayard Presse.

TREGUIER, Eric, *"Comment Préparer Votre Succession", Capital, No. 5, février 1992.*